Children of Dreams

Lorilyn Roberts

All Bible verses are taken from the NIV Study Bible except where otherwise noted.

Children of Dreams by Lorilyn Roberts ISBN 978-1-60264-386-4 (softcover); 978-1-60264-387-1 (hardcover).

Author's Note:
Many of the names in this book have been changed to protect the privacy of the individuals.

To Manisha Hope and Joylin

My

Children of Dreams

ACKNOWLEDGMENTS

Since I had never written a book, I was nervous about "getting it right." I asked friends, family, and brave souls in the "Book Club" at my church for volunteers to read the first draft and several were more than willing to scour the pages in search of "problems." Their honest input has made *Children of Dreams* a much better story, and I am indebted for their encouragement and suggestions.

To the brave Creekside book readers, Mary Lou Shubert, Crystal Castor, and Cari Sue Palmer; to my mom, sister and brother, Paige and Tom; and Doug; my friends, Roger Hunt, Harry Rushing, Laura Lynch, Maureen DeRuyter, Sylvia Murphy, Linsey Murphy, Jenni Murphy, Maureen Syzmansky, Emily Syzmansky, Kris Kirk, Connie Davis, Joyce Davis, Fran Goh, Heather Doles, and Carol DeMar. I feel blessed that you were willing to take your precious time on this project. Thank you!

I also want to thank Joy and Manisha for giving me the time to write. Without their willingness to let me be alone to work and "wing it" for more than a few meals, I couldn't have finished it. Thank you for being so patient.

Most of all, I want to thank my Lord and Savior, Jesus Christ, without whom this book would not be possible. He is the real "author" and "finisher."

Introduction

Hope deferred makes the heart sick, but when dreams come true at last, there is life and joy.

Proverbs 13:12

What does it mean to be adopted? As I look at my two beautiful, internationally adopted daughters, the definition becomes living and full of personal meaning, not just a two-dimensional word on a written page. Maybe what I want is not so much a definition as an understanding of the depths of its meaning on a spiritual level—the act itself of love, sacrifice, cost, and inheritance.

Today my children are ten and seventeen years old and as American as any other child born in this country. We live in middle class suburbia, I drive a "mommy van," our refrigerator is full of too much junk food, my kids wear J.C. Penney clothes, and sleep on comfortable flannel sheets and memory foam pillows. Manisha has Christian teenage friends who come over and watch action-packed movies on our high-definition, forty-eight inch television screen, and Joy competes at level seven on a girls' gymnastics team. We are living the American dream. On the surface, we seem "ordinary," but in reality, we are quite to the contrary.

My two children were orphans from third-world countries. They came from destitute backgrounds without hope, clinging to a miserable existence. I asked my 17-year-old daughter, "What does it mean to you to be adopted?"

"It means I didn't grow in my mommy's stomach but in her heart," she responded.

Sometimes when we decide to write a book, it's because

there isn't a book on the bookshelf that addresses what we want to read. I wanted to understand what it meant to be adopted by my heavenly Father. I searched the Scriptures for all the passages on adoption and thought about what it meant for me personally. The more I thought about it and looked for material, the more I realized how little extra-Biblical literature existed.

I prayed about writing my own book and started writing, but as I wrote, I realized I had to tell my own story. I imagined a beautiful book of how we became a family because I wanted to encourage others to pursue their own dreams of adoption. I wanted it to be a story of hope and fulfillment, but God's adoption of us and the adoption of my children aren't just beautiful adoption stories in the sense that most of us would think of as beautiful.

Mine is the story of the struggle to create a "forever family" as I endured lies, betrayal, sickness, delay, deceit, deception, greed, corruption, suffering, fear, abandonment, and sacrifice. Eventually, through perseverance and dependence on God, I received fulfillment. It soon became clear to me that the adoption of my children wasn't that different from God's adoption of us.

Jesus gave His life for us by paying the ultimate sacrifice at great cost to Himself—suffering on a cruel Roman cross after being abandoned by His closest friends and even God Himself. He suffered every human emotion that I had suffered, but even more so, and without sin.

Perhaps I did accomplish what I wanted, but just not in the way I had originally envisioned. I get teary-eyed when I think about it because I know what heartache and suffering I went through, which pales in comparison to what God has done for us. He has given me a great gift, because I am able to see how much God loves me through the adoption of my children.

In heaven, the Lamb will stand before the throne, in the midst of thousands upon thousands of angels, illuminating us with His holy presence. Only when Jesus breaks the seven seals and opens the scroll, which is the deed to the earth and all its inhabitants, will our entitlement be revealed.

The adoption of my two children was a hard-fought battle—trusting God, forgiving others, and fighting forces of evil that wanted to destroy me. Ephesians 6:10 states:

> Put on the full armor of God so that you can take your stand against the devil's schemes. For our struggle is not against flesh and blood, but against the rulers, against the authorities, against the powers of this dark world, and against the spiritual forces of evil in the heavenly realms. Therefore put on the full armor of God, so that when the day of evil comes, you may be able to stand your ground, and after you have done everything, to stand.

My earthly journey of adoption not only gave me the "Children of Dreams" I longed for, but it has shown me the inheritance awaiting us when we arrive in heaven through God's adoption of us. My story begins many years ago....

The sky receded like a scroll

Revelation 6:14

Chapter One

...and my daughters from the ends of the earth

Isaiah 43:7

April 21, 1994

As the plane soared high above the airport in Seoul, Korea, I stared out the window where the buildings and roads below looked like a child's matchbox set. I felt alone but excited.

A beautiful three-year-old girl, Manisha, was waiting for me in Nepal. I pulled out my only three pictures[1] of her and clasped them tightly. I tried to imagine the moment I would meet her. After eight long years following a painful divorce, would God finally bless me with a daughter?

As we left Korea and headed toward Bangkok, Thailand, the stewardess prepared the trays for dinner. My eyes became heavy as the muffled noise of the plane engine lulled me into a light sleep. Soon I found myself surrounded by stately dark walls and shadows. One voice pierced my heart.

"I took away her dreams."

The words echoed through the judge's chambers carving deep rivets in my soul. The streams of love had long since become a dried riverbed in my husband's heart. The judge paused, taking in my husband's lame confession. He had heard it all before. *Williams vs. Williams* was just one more case on his busy docket. I wished he could assuage my sorrow, but he couldn't.

As the judge signed the divorce decree, I doubted I would ever be happy again. My husband had left me for another woman

---

See back of book for pictures[1]

who carried his child. My dreams of becoming a mother lay in a discarded heap. Thirty years old, childless, and divorced, I was without hope. Feeling like a failure, could I believe God loved me and would heal my broken heart? Did God even care?

I had hit rock bottom and there was no place else to turn. I thought of what Corrie ten Boom once said, "There is no pit so deep but Christ is deeper still." It was her ability to forgive the Nazis after World War II that so impressed me. How could she do that? How could she forgive those who had caused her sister and herself so much pain and humiliation? I desperately wanted children and didn't want to admit that my ex-husband had just taken away my dreams.

Suddenly trays of food jostled by the vibrating of the plane startled me awake. Momentarily forgetting where I was, I glanced around and realized I must have slept.

"Where are we?" I asked the person sitting behind me.

"We are approaching Bangkok."

Wow, I thought to myself. *I really did sleep—like five hours.* It would give me needed energy later, but I also missed dinner and my stomach was empty.

The plane set down on the tarmac in the darkness of night. I disembarked and got far more than I bargained for in Bangkok. I handed the taxi driver at the airport a card with the name of the hotel, the Europa Inn.

The driver nodded his head, and after mumbling a few unintelligible words, loaded my suitcases into his cab for what I thought would be a quick trip to the hotel. However, after an extensive tour of downtown Bangkok, my escort pulled up to a motel in what appeared to be the red light district. Neon lights flashed all around me and signs along the streets displayed seductive advertising. Surely the adoption agency wouldn't have put me up for the night in a seedy hotel.

"This can't be right," I kept trying to tell the taxi driver, feeling uneasy.

He spoke no English and wanted his money.

I waved my hands again trying to explain, "I know this is not the right motel."

He waved his hands back, "No English."

I didn't know what to do. As I stood exhausted contemplating my few options, he proceeded to dump my three huge suitcases out of the taxi. They were far too heavy for me to tote around. I wished I hadn't packed so much, but I knew my problem was far bigger than that.

We had driven for an hour and I needed to be back at the airport in just a few hours. Was I that far away? I looked around to see if I could find someone that spoke English.

I ran into the motel lobby and shouted loudly at the attendant, "Does anybody speak English?" He stared at me blankly. A few raggedly-dressed Thai men were lounging outside the hotel. I hollered to them, "Do you speak English?" They looked at me curiously but didn't say anything.

I ran back to my taxi driver and pleaded with him again, this time more urgently, "I know this isn't right. You've got to take me to the right place. You've brought me to the wrong hotel."

By this time the other Thai men walked over to see what the problem was. The taxi driver and the men carried on a long exchange.

I could see myself the next morning missing my plane because I stayed at the wrong hotel. I could picture in my head trying to explain to the airlines that I needed to catch a later flight. The adoption agency would be upset with me. My contact person would be at the airport to pick me up and I wouldn't be on the plane. I couldn't believe this was happening.

One of the men asked for what I thought was my address. I pulled out my checkbook and gave him a deposit slip. After handing him the slip of paper, I panicked. Why would I give my personal address to somebody that I didn't know? All they wanted was the address of the motel.

After several minutes, the man grabbed my suitcases and motioned for me to get back into the taxi. We took off and drove around again for another thirty minutes before arriving at the "real" Europa Inn.

I breathed a sigh of relief. It was now 1:00 in the morning and my flight would be leaving at 5:30 a.m. Exhausted, I checked into the hotel. The hotel attendant, who spoke English well, assured me I was only a few minutes from the airport.

I finally made it up to my room. After stacking my luggage against the wall, I pulled out a nightgown and headed to the bathroom for a quick shower, but tripped over the uneven ledge. I writhed in pain grasping my toe, agonizing over how I would do the adoption if it was broken.

After a few minutes of a deep massage, I assured myself that it was not broken and a hot shower would fix everything. Later, I tried to imagine what my next day would be like. In just a few hours I would be boarding the plane to fly to Kathmandu, the capital of Nepal.

I closed my eyes and prayed, "Dear Lord, please be with me. Please take away my fear, and keep my dad alive until I return home. Please let nothing happen that could keep me from adopting Manisha."

I had come too far to have something unforeseen stop me. I fell asleep from exhaustion only to be jarred awake just a few hours later.

"Fasten your seat belts," the pilot announced. The no-smoking sign flashed on and the plane engines roared. Soon we would be landing in Kathmandu. My eyes teared up and burned from the lack of sleep. I couldn't believe it was possible to fly so far and still be on the same planet.

After we landed and I exited the plane, I felt as though I had been transported to another world. Huge mountains dotted the countryside. It was a beautiful day, bordering on hot but not unpleasantly so. I took a deep breath as I walked down the tarmac. Cows were lounging between the runways. Old tattered signs marked the entrance to the airport written in a scribble I couldn't read. I was prompted by a young woman showing us the way to customs. No one spoke English. The airport was noisy, crowded, and sweaty.

I felt humanity pressing against me as the surge of passengers from my plane all headed in the same direction. There was a putrid stench in the air—a mixture of unpleasant odors, like an open dumpster that hadn't been emptied for several weeks.

After showing my paperwork and having my passport stamped, I joined another long line of people headed to baggage claims. I stood on my tiptoes to peer over the dark heads and mass of ebony-complexioned travelers. My blonde hair and fair skin made me look like an anomaly. A couple of European or American men toting backpacks were in front. Their masculine build and rough clothes marked them as serious mountain climbers.

Nepal lies between India and China. The country has long been known for its majestic, high mountains and waterfalls that cascade over the rugged terrain. Climbers traveled to Nepal from all over the world to undertake one of the most arduous climbs imaginable, risking their lives to stand atop the world's highest mountain. I hoped to get a picture of Mount Everest as a souvenir.

After I retrieved my bags, I headed toward the front entrance to look for Ankit, my contact person. An Evangelical Christian and pastor in Nepal, he often heard about orphaned children, especially little girls, who had little status in Hindu culture. His desire was to place them in Christian homes in the United States, Canada, and Europe.

People crowded the entrance and I wondered how I would ever find him in the sea of faces. Hastily-written signs shot up everywhere. In the commotion, I looked for a blue and white one that said the name of the adoption agency. I finally saw Ankit and waved my hand. He came over and helped me with my bags, putting them into a waiting taxi. After I was in the taxi, Ankit hopped on his motorcycle and we took off.

As we pulled away from the airport, I was glad to leave behind the discombobulating noise of airplanes, cabs, and travelers. After two days of being airborne, I felt relieved to be on solid ground. We frequently stopped for cows as they stubbornly refused to move and blocked the cab. The countryside was painted in them; most looked emaciated and old. Cows were worshipped and not eaten in Nepal.

The huge mountains surrounding us spoke of unparalleled beauty. Garbage and other debris thrown out of passing cars that reflected in the sunlight were stashed in disheveled piles along the sides of the road. Children in old, torn clothes watched as we drove by. I tried to imagine what Manisha[2], my daughter-to-be, would look like.

"There is the hospital," the taxicab driver said in broken English. He pointed out several other buildings as we went along. I could hardly focus on what he was saying as my mind jumped to what lay ahead. My heart was racing, excited to be here.

After endless turns and one-lane roads, we arrived at the hotel where twelve other adoptive families had stayed. The desk worker recognized us when we entered the hotel lobby.

The Bleu was a plain, four-story, tan-colored brick building in the downtown political district of Kathmandu. A black and white TV played in the small foyer. The floor was well worn and the wall had several coats of cracked paint. Ankit translated for me as I checked in and helped me carry my luggage up the three flights of stairs to my room. There was no elevator.

"After you have a chance to get settled in," he said, "I will meet you downstairs in the lobby in about thirty minutes." Having studied at a Bible College in the Southeastern United States, he spoke English well. "Bring your documents with you," he added, as he closed the door behind him.

After checking out my room, I took my six sets of documents back downstairs and waited for him to return. A few minutes later, he arrived on his motorcycle.

"We need to go to the U.S. Embassy to drop off some paperwork."

I glanced at his motorcycle and stared back at him. I looked down at my new blue skirt and black heels. I didn't want to picture myself riding on a motorcycle with someone I hardly knew dressed in my Sunday attire. I had ridden on a motorcycle only once before in Bermuda many years earlier. What if I dropped the notebook containing all the adoption papers, or worse, fell off?

---

[2] I kept Manisha's Nepali name because of her age and gave her a new middle name, Hope, from Proverbs 13:12

Sensing my concern, he said, "We can rent another taxi, but we'll be doing a lot of traveling in Kathmandu and it will get expensive."

I reluctantly hopped on the back, maneuvering my skirt so it wouldn't clog up the engine. I stuck the heavy black binder between us and wrapped my arms around his waist as tightly as I could. He revved up the engine and we took off down the clogged streets of Kathmandu.

Most people rode on bikes, but every conceivable type of wheeled transport could be seen. Many of the roads were dirt or gravel, and the air was thick with dust. The Nepalis wore scarves and face covers over their nostrils to keep from inhaling the dirt. I didn't have one.

When I arrived back at the Bleu Hotel after our excursion to the U.S. Embassy, my blue skirt was covered in road grime. My skin stung from the debris hurled from the motorcycle and I could taste muck on my lips. The odorous smell of Nepal was now on me. I was repelled and overwhelmed at the same time. I had only been here a few hours and I was already thinking about when I could leave.

One of my suitcases was filled with an assortment of things I had brought to an American family serving as missionaries. The Reeses had been in Kathmandu for quite some time. The mother was a physician, and their children ranged in age from six to twelve. They had called and wanted to know when they could stop by the hotel. The only way they received items from America was when someone brought them. Most mail would not arrive without being pilfered. It had been six months since they had received any packages.

I unloaded my suitcase, wishing I could meet Manisha. Was she in the city? Ankit said we wouldn't be able to see her until tomorrow.

Scattered among the Reeses' things were gifts for Manisha, including a pink doll, Play-Doh, blocks, a yellow toy telephone, and a stuffed dog that made noise when I pushed in his nose. I had also brought a few clothes, some big and some small since I didn't know her size. They were clean and unsoiled by the Nepali air.

The Reeses called and said they would be over in a few minutes. I gathered their things and walked down to the hotel lobby. A short time later they arrived and I was surprised to see three blonde-haired, fair-skinned children show up on bicycles with their father. I wondered how they could seem so American when they lived in such a different culture.

They were excited to receive the gifts. As we sat and chatted in the lobby, an American-looking man walked in with a Nepali girl. I found out he was from Canada and was making plans to return home.

"I got my phone call from India," he explained. "We waited a week. That was the last thing we needed to finish her adoption. We have been here a month."

I felt a twinge of jealousy that they were done and I was just starting. I couldn't imagine being in Nepal for a whole month.

The little girl uttered a few words in Nepali.

"What did she say?" I asked.

The motel attendant said, "She called her father an uncle."

Everyone laughed and I relaxed a little.

"How old is she?"

"She's two," her father said.

I tried to imagine how big Manisha would be compared to her.

"When are you leaving?"

"We are leaving on Tuesday."

So soon; few people spoke English here so my time in Nepal would be lonely. It was reassuring to see that his adoption went through. I hoped mine would be the same. We visited for a few more minutes until the Reeses had to leave.

"I hope to see you again," I told them.

"We'll have you over for an American meal one night," they promised, "and you won't have to worry about the food."

I could look forward to that. I asked them for tips on good restaurants. I had been warned: Don't eat salads, don't eat meat, don't eat vegetables, and don't eat fruit unless it's contained in a peel.

As I left the Bleu Hotel and took my first walk in Kathmandu, I tried to take in the world that opened before my eyes. Poor, dirty, spiritually dark, and oppressive for women, it was a place where hope seemed nonexistent. It was hard for me to believe that my daughter would come from here.

Nepal, home to so many children who would never make it to their fifth birthday; who lived in severe poverty and suffered from lack of nutrition and disease; children who had little hope of ever knowing what it would be like to have a full belly at night or a chance to live life to the fullest. Perhaps most dared to not even dream.

In a country thousands of miles away from my home in Gainesville, Florida, most knew nothing of the God I loved and worshipped. Nepal, a world apart and a world within my heart, the two would be linked forever.

Never again would my heart not skip a beat and my ears not perk up when I heard the name Nepal mentioned in the news. Never again would my mind not be drawn back to these days when I walked its darkened streets.

Chapter Two

For my thoughts are not your thoughts

Isaiah 55:8

I exited the Bleu Hotel, walked a few blocks, and turned left to explore a couple of streets I had not seen. I was careful not to stray too far for fear of becoming lost. Each road looked the same, lined with small, open-air bazaars on each side, with people selling their wares. The tourist trade from Europe and the Middle East helped families eke out a small living. Beautiful silver jewelry hung in the open air along with marionettes used for religious rites.

As the evening drew near, the Nepalis dumped their garbage out along the streets, and the starving cows, now becoming a familiar sight to me, foraged for food from the leftovers. I vacillated between wanting to rub and protect my sleep-deprived eyes from the dirt in the air to not wanting to miss anything, no matter how gross or unsightly. Fascination with the strangeness of the culture whet my appetite to see more.

With shoulder length, wavy, blonde hair and fair skin, I was as much a curiosity to the Nepalis as they were to me. Questioning eyes stared back at me. I represented wealth and money. Shop owners wanted rupees from me to feed their children. Every few minutes a Nepali man would wave at me as if to say, "Come here and buy something."

Nepal is the forty-eighth poorest country in the world. Out of a population of eighteen million, six million drink water we wouldn't give to our dogs. Four years later, I would find out what drinking contaminated water could do to a seven-year-old child.

Trying to ignore the stares, I picked up my pace to find a suitable restaurant.

After a while, all the eating establishments began to look the same and I arbitrarily picked one that seemed friendly. A small sign outside the restaurant written in Nepali displayed their menu. I knew I wouldn't be ordering a hamburger.

I was greeted by a smiling, young Nepali lad who handed me a menu and seated me at a table. The menu was meaningless and the waiter spoke no English. I smiled at him and he smiled at me. At last I pointed to something and he nodded and left. Looking around the dimly-lit restaurant, I was greeted by more stares. Feelings of insecurity crept in as I wondered, sitting all alone, what the future held.

I reflected on how my journey to Nepal really wasn't that unique. I was just a sojourner traveling to a distant land to fulfill what turned out to be only the beginning of my dreams. As the Chinese philosopher Lao Tzu once said, "The journey of a thousand miles begins with one step."

God knew my heart-felt desire was to become a mother. As God longed to have a relationship with me, I wanted a little girl that I could hug, hold, kiss, teach, and spoil. God had promised to wipe away my tears when I met Him in Heaven, but I wanted Him to wipe away my tears now. It was a longing that consumed me, that spoke to my heart with every little girl I saw on the street, in the mall, or in a restaurant.

Did God care about my dreams? Proverbs 13:12 says, "Hope deferred makes the heart sick but when dreams come true at last, there is life and joy." Could I trust God, half a world away, that He would not abandon me? If I left Nepal without the little girl that danced in my dreams and filled me with hope, would I still love God?

My thoughts were interrupted by the waiter laying a tray of food on the table. I couldn't tell what it was in front of me, but I thanked him and smiled to show my approval. He seemed satisfied and proceeded to the next table. I took a few bites and my mind continued to wonder.

I reflected back to some of the events that had brought me to this point. When I was young, my birthfather left my mother and me. I wouldn't meet him again until many years later. Eventually my mother remarried and her new husband, Gene, adopted me when I was ten.

A few years following my painful divorce, I fell in love with a wonderful Christian man, but broke off the engagement when I realized that I was more content to remain single than to marry again. Instead, I poured my energy into obtaining that long elusive college degree. A month following graduation, my adoptive father was diagnosed with a brain tumor. His impending death forced me to examine my own mortality. What would my life be like in ten years? What did I really, really want?

My desire to be a mother remained unfulfilled. No amount of involvement with children at church had quenched my desire and longing to have children of my own. I believed that if God was who He said He was in the Bible, there was no hope, no want no desire, and no dream that was so big that God wasn't bigger still.

Now I sat in a restaurant as different in culture from America as the East is from the West. In Romans 8:37, Paul writes that "...in all these things we are more than conquerors through Him who loved us."

Would Manisha be willing to love and accept me? I was probably the least likely person to adopt a child as a single woman. It would have been hard to find a person more insecure than I was just a few years earlier. I had spent a lifetime believing Satan's lies that I was no good, that I would never amount to anything, that God didn't love me, and that I was unlovable. Unwanted memories would flood my mind, stirring up buried emotions.

I would later meet Manisha in a dingy, dirty motel room halfway around the world. I would bring her out of filth, depravity, and hopelessness for a better life in a new country. She would be given full citizenship and the rights of every other American. She would leave her country of birth for a better place.

Had God not done the same for me? Had He not purchased me with Jesus' shed blood? Did I not long for a better place, an inheritance, where there would be no more pain, sickness, or death? Where my adoption papers were already sealed, waiting for the moment when, as portrayed in Revelation, Jesus would break the seal and open the scroll?

"For my thoughts are not your thoughts, neither are your ways my ways," declares the Lord.

That God chose me, as weak as I am spiritually and mentally, to go to Nepal and adopt a daughter and later adopt a child from Vietnam, is a testament to His faithfulness and unconditional love. I always thought I would have to do something or give up something or suffer something that in my own strength I would cry out, "No, God. I will do anything but that." I had to lay my life down before God could give it back to me.

The rich young ruler was unwilling.

> Jesus looked at him and loved him. "One thing you lack," he said. "Go, sell everything you have and give to the poor, and you will have treasure in heaven. Then come, follow me" (Mark 10:21).

Was it my dream to be a mother that took me to Nepal or was it God's plan for me to adopt Manisha? This side of eternity, I may never know completely, but when I met my daughter for the first time, I knew I was standing on holy ground. Lest I get ahead of myself, night was falling and I needed to return to the Bleu Hotel. I gave what I learned later was a humongous gift for a tip and proceeded on my way.

As I departed, my waiter was immensely pleased, beaming and inviting me to return anytime. Even in his broken English, sign language, and Nepali, it came through clearly that I had made him a rich man, at least for one evening.

Chapter Three

There is a time for everything

Ecclesiastes 3:1

There was so much to do and so little time. If God had made a day to be twenty-five hours long, I could have filled that extra hour up with something. When a woman gets pregnant, she has nine months to prepare for her new bundle of joy. I only had two months.

Our U.S. international adoption laws were never written for the faint of heart. Not only did I have to meet the U.S. international requirements, I had to meet Nepal's requirements as well. Each country has its own set of documentation that must be filled out, submitted, and approved.

I had to fill out an application for an I-600 Petition that permits a person to classify an orphan as an immediate relative, allowing the adoptive parents to bring the child into the country. I had to complete a notarized affidavit of support and provide a copy of my marriage certificate and divorce decree. I had to submit employment letters, plus my 1040 since I was self-employed.

My bank had to provide a certified letter stating what my average balance was for the previous twelve months. I had to show proof of citizenship by providing a certified copy of my birth certificate. I had to type up a cover letter stating I wished to complete filing of my I-600 Petition and attach my fingerprints to the document. I had to have a home study performed by a licensed social worker approving me as a prospective parent. The police department did an abuse registry check to make sure that I didn't have a criminal record. I had to pass a physical and show verification of health insurance. It seems like there was more, but

I blocked it out. I don't want to remember.

With international adoptions, individual countries can open and close adoptions without notice or make changes in requirements. When I initially began the adoption process, I was looking at Guatemala. While gathering my documents, Guatemala closed adoptions and I had to find another adoption agency and country.

After filling out all the required paperwork, I had to make sure my passport was valid so I could travel outside the country. Then I prayed that I would stay sane because I hate filling out documents. International child referrals can take a long time because of the voluminous paperwork, or worse—political upheavals, greed, corruption, baby-selling, and deceitful scams. Sometimes it takes years to jump through all the hoops. For God to accomplish Manisha's adoption in two months was nothing short of miraculous, but then again, we have a God who is in the business of doing what, humanly speaking, seems impossible.

Even before I left, God was taking care of every detail that would require His intervention for Manisha to be my daughter. I had no idea how close I would come to not getting her.

God had always put extraordinary people in my life to accomplish His sovereign purposes. A couple of days before leaving, as I was packing my six sets of documents, I called the Immigration and Naturalization Service in Miami, Florida, to see if they had received my dossier.

"You must be psychic," the woman on the other end of the phone said. "Your packet was just placed in front of me."

"No, I am not psychic. I am a Christian and I think God wants me to adopt this little girl." She wasn't sure what to say to that, so she continued to go through a list of things.

"I don't see your home study," she said.

"They never gave it to me," I told her. "It was mailed by the adoption agency that did my home study, to the adoption agency in the Midwest that was coordinating the Nepali side of things."

"You must have that document," she insisted. "I will overnight a copy of it to you and make sure you take it with you."

The next day, the home study arrived by Fed Ex, and I made

a copy and packed it in my suitcase. Neither adoption agency made sure I had it. A lady from the INS gave it to me overnight by Federal Express.

I could not have adopted Manisha without the home study in my possession.

After dinner and having returned to the Bleu Hotel, I climbed the three flights of stairs to my room and filled out a couple of faxes to let people know I had arrived safely. This was back in the prehistoric days before email. I walked down the stairs again to hand the papers to the receptionist. As I waited for him to finish sending the fax, another Canadian man whom I had not met earlier walked up and gave me one of those looks that makes a woman feel uncomfortable.

I tried to turn away from him, but he persisted, "Why don't you come up to my room tonight..."

I thought I would be nauseous. The last thing I wanted to do was spend an evening with some guy I didn't know. I tried to explain to him I was adopting a little girl, but he had no interest in hearing about that.

I quickly finished my business with the attendant and once again climbed up the three flights of stairs making sure he didn't follow.

Ankit later told me, "You know the wickedness of man. Man is even more wicked here." I had no reason to doubt him. More than once while in Nepal, I felt an evilness that I associated with Hinduism. It was like a coffin being lowered into the ground, a veil covering the truth, the darkness of a bottomless pit full of people with no hope.

Chapter Four

A longing fulfilled is sweet to the soul

Proverbs 13:19

The next morning I awoke at 5:30 a.m. Back home, it was 5:30 p.m.—a twelve-hour time difference. I couldn't go back to sleep, so I got up and took a walk in the opposite direction from the previous day. Shops were beginning to open and people were sweeping the dust off the streets in front of their stores with small hand-held brooms. I grabbed something to eat and arrived back at the hotel about 8:00.

It was Saturday, the only day of the week that Nepalis didn't work. I called Ankit to see if I could attend church with him. I was anxious to meet Manisha and I thought if I was with him, it would speed things along. I also wanted to see what his church was like since he was the pastor.

He arranged to have a taxi pick me up and drop me off at a certain location, and he would take me from there. I carried my Bible in full view thinking I would be thrown in jail, but Ankit had assured me it was okay. I felt awkward toting it around where there were so few Christians. Most of the people in Nepal were either Hindus or Buddhists.

Today as I write, after several years of bloodshed and fighting, Nepal has dissolved its Hindu Monarchy and instituted a Republic. The future is uncertain, much like Russia, which teeters between a pro-western form of democracy and the tyranny of its former despotism. God opens doors for a time in countries, and we must seize the opportunity to be a witness to the Gospel while those doors are open. We never know when those opportunities will close.

After what seemed like a long wait—the world of Nepal exists in slow motion compared to America—Ankit arrived and we traveled a short distance to his church. Located several hundred feet back from the road, it was in a small concrete building that would have been hard to find without his help.

On this sunny Saturday morning in April, a guest speaker from the U.K. delivered the sermon in English with Ankit translating into Nepali. The tall, bearded Englishman was preaching from the Book of Ruth which was written over three thousand years ago. So universal in application, a pastor could preach from it in a different language and culture halfway around the world and have it be as meaningful there as it is here. The message was directed at Nepali Christian students on how to honor their Hindu parents while not sacrificing their Christian testimony.

The men of the congregation sat on one side of the room and the woman sat on the other. There were mats on the floor and fans to keep the building cool as there was no air conditioning.

Before I walked in, I took my shoes off and left them outside the door in a pile with everybody else's. Upon entering, it almost seemed like I was in my own church back home. I could feel God's presence, warm and refreshing, and sense His love among the people. Some in the congregation even spoke a little English as many of the Nepalis were students from the University of Kathmandu.

Ankit introduced me to his wife, his mother, and several other relatives. Almost everyone in Ankit's family was a believer. It was exciting to see what God had done in his life and how so many members of his family had come to know the Lord. There were men, women, children, families, young people, old people, and college students, as well as many visitors.

The service went longer than the typical American church service with a lot of singing and music, and many songs were familiar. In a lot of ways, except for the seating arrangement and bare feet, the order of worship was very similar to my church in Gainesville, Florida. With everything being translated into Nepalese, it went very long. I tried to be patient and attentive. Finally the worship ended and several more people came over to greet me. We chitchatted for a few minutes about my adopting and what it had been like since arriving in Nepal.

Ankit walked me to the door and asked, "Do you want to meet Manisha now?"

There was nothing else I wanted to do more. My heart skipped a beat in anticipation. Suddenly waves of fear swept over me—suppose this meeting went awful? Suppose her father wouldn't give her to me? Suppose I didn't like her? Suppose this was all a big mistake?

The evil one wanted to steal my joy. How many times did I believe his lies? How many times was I hoodwinked into giving up my dreams (the dreams that God gave me)? The only power Satan has is the power to deceive, and too many times I had allowed him to do so.

I had waited too long and traveled too far to listen to him. I believed God was with me and brushed the negative, destructive thoughts aside. I wasn't going to let the evil one have a foothold on this day. As Ankit often said, "These Nepali children have a soul and they need a home where they can come to know Jesus."

I thought of the words to the song "Jesus Loves the Little Children: All the children of the world. Red and yellow, black and white. They are precious in his sight. Jesus loves the little children of the world."

There was a great deal of discussion about how transportation would be handled and the future course of events for the day. It was decided I would ride behind him on his motorcycle in my best Sunday dress, once again, carrying my Bible. We traveled for several blocks through the streets of Kathmandu and were almost to the outskirts of town when we pulled up to another bare concrete building. It looked dirty and rundown.

"I have to go to the bathroom." I could tell that was not what Ankit wanted to hear. My anxiousness had put my kidneys in overdrive, and it had been several hours since I had an opportunity to use the facilities.

He looked at me with one of those knowing looks. "Well, you can go here if you want, but you may not want to." We continued walking around the outside of the building trying to find the entrance, now with even more of a sense of purpose.

Having no luck, Ankit said, "Why don't you wait here and I will go in and try to find it." Eventually he came back out and motioned me into the building. He pointed to the facilities at the end of a dark hallway. I started to walk in, but I could already smell the stench. No matter how badly I needed to go, I would wait.

Ankit later came up with a phrase for my fellow Americans and me, "You Americans are soft."

Moving to the matter at hand, he said, "They are upstairs." We found the stairway and proceeded up. We wandered around on the second floor in the dark because he couldn't remember which room they were in. Eventually he found a door that looked like the right one and knocked. Nothing happened. He knocked again a little louder and still nothing happened.

"I'm sure this is the right room," he whispered. Standing there for a minute not sure what to do, he opened the door and looked in.

"Yeah, she's in there." I was standing beside him and hadn't yet seen inside.

"I want to look in." The wait seemed unbearable.

Ankit stepped aside to allow me to see. I peered in and Manisha was bouncing on one of the beds with just her shirt on. Her father lay straddled across the opposing bed asleep as if he had been up all night.

If I had been writing this scene for a play, there would have been a grand crescendo of music playing right about now, perhaps Vivaldi's "Four Seasons." The plush, velvet curtains would open to a beautifully prepared stage fit for a princess. Everyone would be applauding the momentous, joyous occasion. My fondest moments paled in comparison to this one.

As Jesus was born in a manger without pomp and celebration, giving up His Kingship and heavenly home to become one of us, there was nothing to make this moment seem extraordinary. I was simply a young woman adopting a little girl in a foreign country, nothing that would make the headlines on CNN or Fox News.

The room was barren with no furniture save the two bare

beds with a single white sheet covering them. Not even any drapes to cover the broken windows. No air conditioning to cool the hot, dirty Nepali air. No television, no telephone, no books, and no rugs covered the cold floor. I have no doubt, though, that heaven stirred with excitement and anticipation as one of God's precious little ones would soon be joined with her new mother. Jeremiah 1:5 says: "Before I formed you in the womb I knew you, before you were born I set you apart…"

Chapter Five

...the greatest of these is love

I Corinthians 13:13

Ankit nudged me back so he could shut the door. He knocked several times loudly to wake up the father. We finally heard stirring in the room and he came to the door. He partially opened it and smiled at both of us, motioning for us to come in. He and Ankit exchanged a few words in Nepali. I eased my way into the room and sat down on the bed opposite where Manisha had been jumping. There was an awkward moment of silence. I wanted Manisha's father to put some clothes on his daughter.

I asked Ankit to ask him if he had any clothes for her. Raj, her father, smiled politely and grabbed a pair of blue, ragged-looking denim trousers. They were well-worn and dirty, about three sizes too big, but I was glad for anything.

Manisha was playful and warm. Her face was more light complexioned than her arms and legs, which looked dry from lack of good nutrition. She had round, deep brown eyes. Nepalis look more Indian than Chinese. Her father pulled out of his pocket what appeared to be a small bottle of oil and stroked some of it into her short, straight, dark brown hair. I wondered why he had done that.

She turned her attention to Ankit and they played a silly game. She pretended to hide something she had made into a toy. I felt left out but enjoyed watching them, impressed at how happy and content she was.

There were no toys or snacks in the room. There was nothing for her to entertain herself with, but she had made a toy and was happy to share it with us.

After a while, I got up the nerve to ask if I could hold her.

Her father smiled and nodded. A warm and engaging person, I would learn later Manisha was much like him. He was about my height in stature with curly dark hair and glasses. His glasses were the most noticeable feature besides his smile. I immediately took a liking to him.

Ankit passed Manisha over to me and I held her in my lap. I couldn't believe how light she was. She was tiny for three years at twenty-three pounds. She laughed and giggled as I bounced her on my knee. Ankit and Raj watched intently which made me nervous. I asked if I could walk around with her outside. They both said, "Yes, that would be good."

I picked her up and we walked down the stairs. As we stepped outside, the sun's rays enveloped us in a severe brightness after being in the dark building. Some nearby birds sang a whimsical melody of enchantment. I was smitten by love! Alone at last with my new daughter, I was overcome with emotion. I walked over to some flowers and pointed to one and said "flower." I picked it off and gave it to her. We walked around the building several times. I pointed to the chirping birds and said "bird." The few minutes with her in my arms seemed like a dream from which I didn't want to awake. She was content and beaming.

Because she didn't speak English and I didn't speak Nepali, I gazed into her eyes and tried to imagine what she might be thinking. Did she have any idea who I was? I did not know what her father had told her. I longed to talk to her but I would have to be patient. Most of all, I wanted to remember how special the day was.

On this day, as we picked flowers, admired the birds, and basked in each other's company for the first time, I realized that God had heard my cries for a daughter.

"...what hath God wrought" (Numbers 23:23)!

After a while, Raj and Ankit came outside. They had been discussing plans. I started to realize how late it was in the day and how hungry I was.

"Could we get something to eat?" I asked.

Neither Ankit nor Raj seemed particularly interested in food. They were talking about documents and legal things that needed attention. Tiredness was on the verge of sapping the last ounce of energy within me. I needed to eat something.

After much discussion in Nepali, Ankit translated.

"We're going to go to my house and get some papers and documents signed."

I acquiesced without any more mention of food. At least I could use the bathroom. He flagged down a taxi for Manisha and me to ride in and Raj rode behind Ankit on his motorcycle. Manisha seemed content to stay with me rather than her father, so I was happy to keep her.

We arrived at Ankit's house and he took us up some stairs to one of the bedrooms. I sat down on the wooden floor and they sat on the bed. Ankit was holding a folder with some papers. Manisha, like any active three-year-old, wanted to run around. So I set her down and she ran out into the hallway.

I could hear a woman's voice talking to her. It was fretful that I couldn't understand so much of what was being said.

Ankit spoke English well and would translate for me when I looked at him questioningly. Apparently Manisha didn't like the picture of the white monkey in the hallway, so it was promptly removed.

Now that we were here and things had settled down, I told him again I needed to use the facilities. He called for one of the ladies in the home and she came and took me to the bathroom.

"Thank you," I said politely, not knowing whether she understood me or not, only to discover as I closed the door there was no toilet paper.

Sheepishly and somewhat embarrassed, I went back to Ankit.

"There isn't any toilet tissue." I would have preferred to have told one of the women, but I didn't think they spoke English.

In typical Nepalese inflection, he translated into Nepali for one of the women to bring me some toilet paper. By now my stomach was really hurting. So I asked if they could also bring me some food.

After I used the facilities, I saw they had brought me a couple of crackers and a glass of water. I focused on the water and all I could think was what I had been told before I left home.

Don't drink any water unless it's in a bottle.

Again, I went back to Ankit, "Do you have any bottled water?"

"No," he said. "We don't have any bottled water."

There ensued a great deal of discussion in Nepali. I felt like I had caused everybody a great deal of inconvenience, but after a while, another young lady showed up with some bottled water. I thanked her as best I could.

I thought to myself, *Lori, try not to cause any more trouble. You have caused enough for one day.*

On a more personal note, I wondered, do they not use toilet paper around here? What about when it's that time of the month?

I know, too much information.

After a few bites of food, I made myself comfortable on the floor. Ankit handed me what seemed like volumes of documents. Unfortunately I had never been good at filling out papers. I made several errors and could tell he was a little upset. He left the room to retrieve something akin to white-out to blot out all of my mistakes, mumbling something to the effect, "It's important to not make mistakes on the documents."

There were too many papers. I did not feel like answering any more questions. I was preoccupied with watching Manisha and her father. Everyone was talking in Nepali as I continued to fill in blanks.

There were a lot of personal questions.

"Do I have to answer all of this?" I asked.

Ankit explained, "You did the American side in the States. Now you have to do the Nepali side."

I had no idea what was in store for me. This was just the beginning.

After what seemed like a long time, I finished answering everything.

Ankit asked me, "Would you like to take Manisha with you? It's okay with the father."

I glanced at him who nodded approvingly.

After a few seconds, however, I realized how stressed and tired I was. Jet lag was beginning to take its toll and I knew I needed another day.

"I think I should wait till tomorrow. I need a good night's sleep."

Chapter Six

...I will fear no evil, for you are with me

Psalms 23:4

On March 15, 1994, at the end of the child referral letter I received from the adoption agency was this paragraph:

> Any family adopting Manisha will be required to travel to her native village in Janakpur to obtain signed paperwork from the village mayor and Chief District Officer. This district is accessible by plane, car, and foot. It is a remote, rural district isolated from medical and other facilities. There may be no heat, running water, or electricity. The location and isolation of this district places any individual or family at increased risk for accidents, disease, and even death, prepared by the director and placement supervisor.

Today, as I reread the paragraph above from the adoption agency, I am reminded of my fear that night at the Bleu Hotel.

Romans 8:15 says: "For you did not receive a spirit that makes you a slave again to fear, but you received the Spirit of sonship. And by him we cry, Abba, Father."

Why would God contrast a spirit of fear with the spirit of adoption? I knew God wanted me to adopt Manisha so why was I so fearful? Upon arriving back at my hotel room later that night, I succumbed to overwhelming fatigue. I laid my head on the pillow bemoaning my weakness. *I didn't have what it took to be a single mother,* I cried.

Halfway around the world all alone in a country and culture completely different from America, I wondered if I had made a terrible mistake. Could I take a child whom I had just met, who didn't look anything like me, and promise her, you are mine forever? Was I willing to spend twelve hours in a van the next day on a one-lane, half-paved road with strangers speaking a language I didn't understand? Could I eat strange food and not worry about the guards that Silas warned might stop or search us? What about my fear of heights as we traveled atop the highest mountains in the world on a road that wind like a corkscrew to China?

I felt dizzy thinking about what lay ahead of me, as if I was a minute droplet amongst millions cascading over the steep Himalayans into streams thousands of feet below. Could I handle seeing starving children with red hair and distended bellies, images that would sear my conscience forever, knowing I could only save one?

"Oh, God," I cried out, "please help me not to be afraid." I was too overwhelmed to read my Bible. The lack of sleep made even the simplest of logic seem impossible. I wasn't sure I could go through with it. Would God be sufficient in my hour of greatest need?

But even this didn't compare to my fear a few years earlier scuba diving in the waters off the Turneffe Islands.

The Turneffe Islands are the largest of three atolls consisting of over two hundred mangrove islands thirty-five miles off the coast of Belize City. Not only is it a diver's paradise, but after leaving Belize City for the three-hour jaunt in a small boat, it becomes a complete escape from the busyness of our chaotic world. There are no TVs, no computers, no telephones, no radios, and no newspapers.

One morning we went out on what is called a "drift dive." A drift dive is where the diver jumps off the side of the boat and the current carries him either on a harrowing rollercoaster ride or a meandering, leisurely tour.

Drift diving was my favorite kind of dive because I didn't have to worry about where the dive boat was. I was never adept at using a compass under water. With drift diving, the dive boat follows the "bubbles" and picks up divers when they float to the surface.

On this day I jumped off the boat and went down like a weighted anchor. Rather than floating lazily in the current, I found myself within a few seconds at eighty feet deep. I was quite impressed that I beat everyone else down. Usually my dive buddy would have to wait on me because scar tissue in my left ear made it difficult for me to equalize. All alone, I moseyed around for a few minutes waiting for the other divers to float down beside me, but no one showed up. It was a beautiful dive and I didn't want to cut it short by heading to the surface, but divers aren't supposed to swim alone in the ocean. Actually, it's a foolish thing to do, so reluctantly, I went to the surface.

When I poked my head out and looked around, the only boats in sight were way off in the distance. The dive boat had left me behind, following the other divers on their drift. I was all alone in the Gulf of Mexico with a 40-pound tank on my back in the middle of nowhere. I knew it would take an hour for the others to finish their dive and decompress, depending on how deep they went. They would have to get back on the boat and discover I was missing. I figured it would be at least a couple of hours before I would be rescued if I was ever rescued at all.

The first hour floating all alone in the ocean I remained calm. The second hour gave way to waves of fear and panic as I began to seriously ponder my desperate situation. *Suppose the dive boat never found me?* My life passed before my eyes. What a horrible way to die. I wasn't ready. "Please, God," I cried out, "don't leave me out here in the Gulf. I want to live."

I contemplated what few options I had, which were none, and thought about how many sharks might be lurking. What was underneath my dangling feet and would I ever be found? I floated helplessly for hours with a forty-pound tank on my back breathing though my snorkel in the middle of nowhere.

Had God not saved my life that day in the Turneffe Islands for something far more wonderful than I could have imagined? Would I let Satan rob me of my joy of adoption by filling my heart with fear? I was tired, hungry, and emotionally drained. Satan knew I was vulnerable.

Only God could take away my slavery to the fear that paralyzed me. As fear's grip on me let go, God held me in His arms, much like a mother would hold her infant daughter, and spoke silently to my heart, "I love you."

At last, I peacefully dozed off. I awakened early the next morning feeling strong and courageous, anxious to get on the road and ready for an incredible adventure. Never again in the years since have I doubted that Manisha was supposed to be my daughter. I was filled with peace, had a good night's rest, and was ready for whatever storms lay ahead.

We would be leaving at 5:30 a.m. to travel to the Janakpur District to have documents signed by the CDO. It would be a long and arduous journey.

Chapter Seven

...let us go up to the mountain of the Lord

Micah 4:2

I ate a light breakfast at the small restaurant inside the Bleu Hotel, consisting of tea and toast. I made sure everything was packed for the trip, including nuts, bananas, and candy bars.

"You have to feed everybody for the trip," Ankit said. "There will be five of us."

I triple checked that I packed all six sets of documents and that everything was in order. I was anxious to get going and was impatient for him to show up.

At last, he arrived at the hotel wearing jeans, a light jacket, and a red cap, along with the driver in a white van. It was barely light outside and quiet. The streets were empty and the stores had not yet open. I was surprised that Manisha and her father weren't in the van.

"We'll pick them up on the way out of town," Ankit reassured me. I wondered if Manisha had anything to eat. If not, she could fill up on all the snacks I brought. I showed Ankit the food and we both climbed into the van.

Wearing a blue dress and white blouse, I was glad to be spared another motorcycle ride. I loaded a fresh roll of film in my Nikon camera and made sure I had plenty of money to pay the driver. My paranoia prompted me to check once again that I wasn't missing any documents.

I looked forward to getting out of Kathmandu for the day (the dusty air was bothering my sinuses) and seeing the beautiful countryside and towering Himalayan Mountains.

"Be sure to bring your camera," Ankit said. "You will get a

good view of Mount Everest if it's not cloudy."

It took a while to travel through downtown Kathmandu. The sun was just beginning to cast its first rays of light over the streets and buildings, and I could see shadows of people in the distance.

I was startled to see so many standing on the edge of small streams by the road brushing their teeth. The water appeared muddied from the rains. I had noticed a toothbrush and toothpaste in the hotel room when I met Manisha. For a country that didn't seem to use toilet paper, it surprised me that anyone would brush their teeth.

Ankit exited the van and walked into the hotel to retrieve Raj and Manisha. Eventually they made their way out and I saw that Manisha was wearing the same dirty blue outfit from the previous day. My heart ached to put something new on her. I imagined how beautiful she would look in the pretty pink dress and checkered blue top I brought her.

They climbed into the van and Raj smiled at me. Manisha was quiet and did not want to sit beside me today. She stayed with her father. I asked Ankit to ask Raj if she had eaten.

"A glass of milk," he replied. I felt badly as I had eaten more than she had.

After a while we left Kathmandu far behind. Old brick and concrete buildings were replaced with scenic flowers and grass, with clumps of trees dotting the countryside. Every so often we passed young lads shepherding cows on the side of the road. Grass took over where there had been dirt and scenic rolling hills followed one after another in an orderly, rhythmic pattern. The panoramic vistas, the motion of the van, and lack of sleep made the trip seem dream-like, but I was jolted back to reality by the start and stop of the steady stream of vehicles ahead of us and those coming from the opposite direction.

As the day went on, the road deteriorated into one bump after another. Eventually the two-lane road narrowed to one, and the rolling hills out of Kathmandu became gigantic mountains. The road wound like a child's slinky, and I wondered at every turn if someone approaching from the other side would hurl us into the abyss below. Around every bend I heard horns honking, ours or another car, and sometimes both.

Our destination was the Dolakha District of the Janakpur Zone, the town of Charikot. Our trek took us from Lamusagu, which was about 47 miles outside of Kathmandu, to Lamosagu Jiri, another 27 miles. Then we traveled to Khaktapur, which had been the main trade route for centuries between Tibet/China and India. That accounted for the high volume of traffic. Its position on the main caravan route made the city rich and prosperous by Nepali standards.

The scenery was spectacular. Never had I seen such incredible beauty. We were surrounded by mountains in every direction as far as the eye could see. I wondered how such incredible beauty could coexist side by side with some of the most destitute people in the world. If it weren't for the children who were so malnourished, with protruding bellies and red hair, I could have been totally absorbed in the magnificence of the Himalayans, but the children were heartbreaking.

Nepal's per capital income was only $180 per year, one of the lowest in the world and the lowest in South Asia, where the average per capital income was $350 per year. Of its eighteen million inhabitants, half lived in abject poverty.

The next town was Dolalghat, where we crossed a long bridge over the Tamakosi River, which was about six hours from Kathmandu.

We subsequently came upon the Indrawati River where a large group of people were gathered, facing an unusual construction of wood in the middle of the river. It was still smoldering from being burned.

"What is that?" I asked Ankit.

"They are having a funeral. It is the Hindu custom to burn the dead body over a river."

I hated thinking about Manisha's birthmother in that way.

"Just down the river a little further," he continued, "at Chere, we recently baptized about twenty people."

I chose to focus on the baptism of believers in the river rather than the burning of dead bodies for the rest of the trip to Janakpur.

We traveled along the Bhotekosi River and crossed that river at Khardi Sanopakhar, Dada Pakhar, and Thulopakhar, which was close to Ankit's village.

Then we came to Sildhunga, Mude, and Kharidhunga, which were nine thousand feet above sea level. After that, we traveled through Boch, and finally arrived at Charikot, which was the district headquarters of the Dolakha District in Janakpur, arriving in the late afternoon. Januk was the name of a famous king and "pur" means city or town. It was a historical holy city.

As we were driving along and the road became nearly intolerable to ride on, I looked at Manisha and wondered how she could not get sick. I shouldn't have thought it because soon thereafter, she threw up. Her father tried to hold her out the window as we were driving until the last of the milk landed on the road instead of in the van. Maybe it was a good thing she only had milk for breakfast. She looked dreadfully unhappy. If only I had brought a change of clothes for her.

After a long while, we stopped. Everybody got out and walked in different directions. I wasn't sure what I was supposed to do.

Ankit glanced back at me and said, "It's time to go to the bathroom."

I convinced myself I didn't need to go. Maybe if I waited a while, we would come to a restaurant somewhere, like a McDonald's, and I could go then. Of course, there was nothing but mountains around us in the middle of the Himalayans. I just wasn't ready to head for the bushes.

"I don't need to go," I lied, waiting in the van while everyone else disappeared. Plus, I didn't bring any toilet paper. D___ that toilet paper. As I looked out the window, a female monkey in season scurried by the van.

I had a few moments to be captivated by the view. There was nothing around me but mountain peaks adorned in various shades of blue and green. I wondered how there could be so much evil, so much violence, so much wrong with the world when so far from all of that, God's handiwork stood tall and majestic. It was like God had painted the sky, the mountains, the rivers and waterfalls with a touch of heaven, a glimpse of what awaits us beyond heaven's gates. The mountains and the trees and fields would have burst forth in praise if it were possible.

The beauty was like a tiny thread woven through a tapestry where time and sin had ravaged the perfect nature of all things; one lone thread that promised redemption, a taste, if you will, of the magnificence of God's original creation.

Within me a sense of longing arose, a burning desire to partake of the beauty of our heavenly home that God is preparing for us. Whatever my eyes have beheld here, that my senses have been awakened to, so much more so will it be there. Paul wrote in I Corinthians 2:9, "... as it is written: 'No eye has seen, no ear has heard, no mind has conceived what God has prepared for those who love Him.'"

Eventually everyone returned to the van. Manisha and her father climbed in sitting to the left of me in the back. She had warmed up to me again and I was able to hold her for a few minutes as the van gathered speed on the half-paved, half-dirt road.

Her clothes now were not only dirtied and soiled, but smelled of sour milk. Her shoes, riddled with holes and far too small, had been tossed into the back of the van.

It was still hard for me to believe she was going to be my daughter. I would rest easier when we were in the air over Kathmandu headed toward Los Angeles. That seemed an eternity away right now. There was lots of talk going on but since everyone spoke in Nepali, I didn't know what was being said except for the occasional translation by Ankit.

We continued to travel for a long time passing through small villages where we had to make numerous stops to register with an official who sat in a hut beside the road.

A couple more hours passed and no McDonald's or Wendy's showed up on the radar, so I thought before things got desperate, I better do something. There were too many jolts of the van on the bumpy road to wait too long.

Ankit asked the driver to stop and a few minutes later he pulled the van over to the side of the road.

"Is this okay?" Ankit asked.

"Well, I don't have any toilet paper."

He looked back at me in amazement. "Why didn't you bring

toilet paper?"

"I didn't know I would need toilet paper. I just thought we would stop somewhere at a restaurant and go."

"We're out in the middle of the Himalayan Mountains!"

There were no restaurants out here, just mountains and small make-shift homes with poor, needy children running around taking care of cows more dead than alive, and one monkey in heat. No five-star hotels, let alone anything resembling a Western-style restaurant.

"We'll stop at the next village and I'll try to get some," Ankit said.

Guys just don't get it, I thought. Or maybe I really am a soft American.

Later we made a brief stop at a little shack in a small village. Ankit ran in and purchased some toilet paper, quickly came out, and handed it to me through the window. I tried not to look embarrassed and avoided eye contact with everybody. I was just glad to have my toilet paper.

We proceeded to drive along the road and every few minutes the driver slowed down and Ankit would look back at me with a questioning look, "Is this a good place to stop? Do you want to stop here?"

"Yeah, this is okay," I said at last. I just wanted to be done with it.

I climbed out of the van and started heading down a little path off to the side of the road carrying my toilet paper mumbling to myself, "I am not a soft American girl. Gee, they probably do this all the time."

After doing my deed I headed back up the trail and saw that everyone else had left the van. Fortunately nobody went my way, so I just waited until everybody returned.

By now we were all hungry so I handed out some of the snacks that I brought and we began to munch on them. It was about 3:00 or so in the afternoon when we finally arrived at the CDO's office.

We pulled off the road to a large open area in front of a two-story, white concrete building with brown shutters. A red and white Nepali flag hung limply from a flag post out front.

There were a few children and men milling about. It was quiet and peaceful, unlike the bustle of activity in Kathmandu. The whole area was surrounded by mountains off in the distance.

As I looked toward the east, Ankit said, "Just over those mountains is China." It felt like the ends of the earth. I took a few pictures and then followed Ankit up the flight of stairs to the second story of the CDO's office. Manisha and her father followed closely behind. I clasped my documents under my arm and held on to them nervously.

"You need to be friendly with the CDO and talk to him when he asks you questions." I could tell Ankit was also nervous.

Appearing in front of a government official who wielded such power over my future was certainly out of my bailiwick. I tried to focus on the matter at hand but my heart was racing, wanting it to be done. My throat was so dry I wasn't even sure I could respond to any questions he might ask me.

As we stood in the doorway, the room appeared very dark. We were motioned in and I found an empty seat several feet from the door. As I waited for my eyes to adjust, I gazed through the window. The Himalayan Mountains in the distance seemed to symbolize the huge hurdle in front of me in the guise of this official.

Manisha sat beside me. One exposed light bulb with wires crisscrossing the ceiling provided the only lighting. Old wooden chairs lined the bare walls. I felt like I was starring in a movie as I sat in the dusty, dingy office of the CDO of Dolakha, Nepal.

A man in his early 30's, the CDO was dressed in a green suit with a pointed little cap on top of his head. It was hard to comprehend how a man on the other side of the world could have such incredible control over my destiny except God had given him that authority.

My thoughts flashed back momentarily to all that preceded this defining moment in my life. As a child my parents told me I was born under a cloud. My husband chided me, "Is this another one of your sad stories?"

"I don't love you anymore," my partner spitefully responded one night after I presented him with evidence that he was seeing another woman. I remembered the wine bottles and cheese that I uncovered in the garbage after being away for a few days visiting my family.

I replayed scenes of the long hours I worked as a court reporter putting him through medical school. I recalled the night he contacted the police after I confronted him in his office at the hospital. Two weeks after our divorce was final, the other woman gave birth to his child. I was devastated and hurt. Only a loving God could help me to recover and begin a new life in Him. Would God give me a chance to redeem the years the locusts had eaten?

A few years after my divorce, I received a letter from World Vision, an evangelical organization that sponsors children in Third World countries. The beginning of the letter, dated February 13, 1993, read: "Over 150 million children worldwide are trapped by hunger, sickness, poverty, and neglect." I took the letter and put it on my refrigerator. *Someday,* I thought, *I am going to adopt a child from another country.* How and when, only God knew.

The letter ended with the quote from Proverbs 13:12 (LB): "Hope deferred makes the heart sick, but when dreams come true at last, there is life and joy."

I looked at Manisha and reflected on what the future would hold. With her piercing, dark brown eyes focused on me, she spoke softly in clear English, "I love you."

I responded back, "I love you, too."

I did not know how she could have uttered those words because she could not speak English. I thought about what the Bible said concerning speaking in tongues and wondered if I had witnessed another one of God's miracles. Whether I could explain it or not, it gave me the assurance I needed over the next few days that God was in control.

As we sat and waited, there was a lot of talk in Nepali.

The CDO asked Ankit a few questions as various men walked in and out handing him papers to sign.

He continued to pour over my documents and after awhile looked up and asked, "You're not forty?"

"No," I said, "but I'm almost forty."

"It's the law you must be forty." He gave a cursory glance through the rest of my papers. He and Ankit exchanged a flurry of words in Nepali. Some elderly men sitting in the room stared at me. I had the feeling that Ankit was talking about my infertility. I felt exposed that such personal information was being bantered about. I saw worry in Ankit's eyes and knew my hopes of becoming a mother were precariously in limbo.

Ankit and the CDO continued to talk for a while longer. I went and sat by him hoping for some reassurance. More old men came in and the CDO turned his attention to other matters. About this time, Manisha's father, not happy with the sudden turn of events, took Manisha outside and I could hear her running up and down the wooden planks.

Ankit said to me in a whisper, "The CDO said he cannot approve your adoption because you're not forty, and he has to abide by the law. He is putting in a call to the legal office in Kathmandu to see if they will give him permission but they won't do it. We will have to go ourselves and meet with the Home Minister after we get back to Kathmandu."

We continued to wait for a long time for the phone call. Finally the phone rang and the CDO talked loudly on the phone. When he got off, they discussed the call. I could tell it wasn't good.

Ankit shook his head indicating that he could not get permission to sign my paperwork.

"I wish I could do your adoption, but I can't," the CDO told me in broken English.

I knew it wasn't his fault. He had tried. I had known before I came to Nepal about the age forty rule, but what difference did it make in my case because I couldn't get pregnant? Written laws prohibiting a child from having a home, a future, and a hope— why, God?

Manisha was an orphan; her mother had died when she was a baby, and her father couldn't support her. He didn't want to support her. Girls were considered a liability in Hindu culture and without her birthmother, the life she faced was one of destitution and death.

This road seemed so familiar to me. I had walked it before,

more than once; loss, separation, and abandonment. I cried out, "Not here, Lord, not in Nepal. A three-year-old orphan girl needs a chance to know You."

Chapter Eight

...ask the animals, and they will teach you

Job 12:7

My mind flashed back to when I was young. I was awakened by a big white dog licking me in my face and jumping all over my bed. As I tried to open my eyes from what I thought was a dream, my mother said, "This is Gypsy. We are going to keep her."

Gypsy was the friend I longed for but didn't have. When I came home from school, she would greet me at the door with her tail wagging. I walked her, fed her, and played with her. After we returned from each walk, I would announce how many times she had used the bathroom, both number one and number two, as if to validate I was the best dog walker in the world. I even cleaned up after her when she threw up so nobody would know.

Gypsy was a stray. The night before she jumped on me in bed she had snuck into the house with my dad. She was God's gift to me. We were inseparable.

One afternoon I arrived home from school and knew something was wrong. She didn't greet me at the door like she usually did and I ran through the house frantically looking for her.

"She's gone," my mother and father told me. "She won't be back. The manager of the apartment came and took her away."

"Where did they take her?" I cried.

"The manager said they would dump her off on the road somewhere far from here. You know the apartment complex doesn't allow dogs."

I ran out of the room and up the stairs to my bedroom. My mind was flooded with memories of the most important thing in my little world. My heart was broken, confused, and hurting. Gypsy was gone.

That night bolts of thunder crashed outside my bedroom. Lightning pierced through the window shades. I imagined Gypsy in the darkness. I could feel her white warm fur against my skin and see her dark, brown eyes pleading for me to come get her. I cried into my pillow as peels of thunder bounced off the walls. If Gypsy ever found her way back, I vowed to run away with her. I would never let anybody take her from me again.

But the next day came and went and she didn't return. I went to school each day hoping for the impossible, that somehow she could find her way back from wherever they dumped her.

It was Wednesday, the day before Thanksgiving. We were packing things up to go visit my new father's family in North Carolina. My mother had recently remarried. I kept looking up the hill in front of the apartment, imagining that she would come running down the street any minute. I knew it would be impossible, but still I hoped. I made one last trip to my bedroom. The car was loaded and we were ready to leave. I picked up my pillow and thought of the first morning she licked me on the face in bed.

"Please, Gypsy, come back to me. You need a home and someone to love you. I need you."

I walked out the door of our apartment to get into the car. I glanced one last time up the hill. Out of nowhere, suddenly, there was something white. Was it, could it be—I dropped my pillow and started running up the hill. I ran as fast as my legs would carry me, my mind racing to think what seemed like the impossible. It couldn't be—but it was.

Gypsy ran frantically toward me, tattered, dirty, and exhausted. Somehow she had miraculously found her way home through the raging storm. After being lost for days in the cold November nights, miles from our home, Gypsy had done the impossible. She had found her way back to me.

"Gypsy!" I cried. I crouched down to grab her as she jumped into my arms, holding her tightly around the neck, crying and rejoicing all at the same time. My dog was lost, but now she was found.

"I will never let go of you," I promised. She squealed with delight and licked my face. For the first time in my young life, I knew there had to be a God.

Chapter Nine

...weeping may remain for the night

Psalm 30:5

Does God not take care of orphans and widows? In John 14:18 Jesus promised that "I will not leave you as orphans. I will come to you."

Surely God would not abandon Manisha, leaving her here in Nepal where she would never hear of the Savior's love. If God was able to reunite a little girl with her beloved dog against all odds, if God could become the husband for a young wife abandoned by her unfaithful husband, if God was my heavenly Father who had promised to never leave me or forsake me, surely He wouldn't abandon me now.

God, who knows every hair on my head, who knows everything about me and loves me anyway, who sacrificed His only Son so I could have eternal life with Him, could I not render unto God what was God's and render unto Caesar what was Caesar's? Did God not put the authorities in power in Nepal? Did not the winds and sea obey Him?

When everything seemed hopeless, could I believe that God is the Great Shepherd who never abandons His sheep?

In John 10:11, Jesus says, "I am the good shepherd. The good shepherd lays down His life for the sheep."

For this is what the Sovereign Lord says: I myself will search for my sheep and look after them. As a shepherd looks after his scattered flock when he is with them, so will I look after my sheep. I will rescue them from all the places where they were scattered on a day of clouds and darkness. I will bring them out from the nations and gather them from the countries and I will bring them into their own land (Ezekiel 34:11-13).

I reflected back to what Manisha said to me shortly before the CDO said he couldn't approve the adoption, "I love you." It was as if God had said to me, "I love you."

The trip back to Kathmandu was emotionally difficult. We arrived just after dusk. Manisha had thrown up two more times in the van. She needed a mother's comfort and touch to clean her up and make her feel loved. Her old, thread-bare shoes looked like they had been used by a half-dozen kids. I longed to be her mother, to bathe her, to give her a new dress and a bright pair of brand-new shoes she could show off, but it wasn't meant to be this night.

The most I could hope was for her dad to take some things I had brought and give them to her. I picked out a pink corduroy dress and blue checkered shirt that I knew would fit her. I also handed him a pretty nightgown and underwear. But he did not know what they were for and I didn't know how to explain it to him. The little girls of Nepal did not wear nightgowns or panties to bed. They were too poor.

I said good night to both of them. As they left for Ankit to drive them back to their hotel, I closed the door and realized how totally exhausted I was. All I wanted to do was sleep.

The next morning arrived. I heard stirring on the street four stories below with the first rays of sunlight peeking through the window. I had become accustomed to hearing people throw up every morning as the hotel walls were thin and betrayed more than I cared to know.

I wanted today to be different. I found a new place to eat where the food promised to be more appetizing. There appeared to be more Westerners and Europeans here. I had yet to run into another American.

Later in the morning following breakfast, I heard a knock on my door. I opened it and Manisha stood by her father with a broad smile and eyes sparkling like diamonds. Even in my troubled heart, I felt swept off my feet as she modeled her new outfit. Far from her home where she wore ragged clothes and shoes, she had become a princess. Rags to riches in a day, fairy tale stories still happen. I wanted this one to end with her knowing her King.

Earlier I had called my mother and asked for prayer. Isaiah 34:5-6 came to mind, "Do not be afraid, for I am with you. I will bring your children from the east and my daughters from the ends of the earth."

"O, Dear God," I prayed again, "Please let this be Your will. Please give me the desires of my heart." I had dressed up, too, waiting for Ankit to come and take me to the Home Minister.

He arrived a little later and we had a big discussion about whether to take his motorcycle or a taxi. I was all dressed up and didn't want to ride on a motorcycle. He hated spending so much money for rides even though it was my money, but every time I rode on a motorcycle, I was covered with dirt. I prevailed this time. We hired a taxi.

As we traveled to the Legal Office, he warned me, "The Home Minister is directly underneath the Prime Minister. Try to make a good impression."

The courthouse and government buildings were located in the heart of downtown Kathmandu. A tall, white wall surrounded the entire complex. The taxi dropped us off outside the walled entrance and we walked inside to the legal office of the Home Ministry. It was a beautiful day. The sun's rays lifted my spirits as if God's radiance shown upon me, but Ankit was uncomfortable.

"They don't like me in the legal office," he said. "I refuse to pay them money for the adoptions."

Bribery is what they call it in America. Although illegal even in Nepal, with some adoption facilitators it happened all the time.

As we sat patiently waiting, nobody went out of their way to help us. Ankit eventually engaged a male secretary at the front desk in conversation, and he motioned us into another room.

There followed a lot of talk in Nepali. I knew that whatever happened there would be no bribes and no money to pay anyone off. God would have to intervene and make it possible for me to adopt Manisha.

I prayed quietly for God to move on the Home Minister's heart. An errand boy, after an extended discussion with Ankit,

47

went into his office. We waited until he reappeared. Speaking in Nepali, he relayed the Home Minister's decision.

Ankit breathed a sigh of relief and anticipation.

"The Home Minister has said it's okay for you to adopt Manisha."

My eyes filled with tears as I remembered Manisha's softly-spoken words in the Himalayan Mountains, "I love you."

God had given me a daughter from the ends of the earth. He would restore the years the locusts had eaten.

Sher Bahadur Deuba, the Home Minister, later became Prime Minister of Nepal on three separate occasions. I can't underestimate the power of prayer and that it is God who moves in the hearts of kings and leaders to do His bidding.

Chapter Ten

...a time of happiness and joy, gladness and honor

Esther 8:16

It would take a couple of days to process the paperwork. We would have to travel back to the Dolakha District and meet once again with the CDO to have him sign his part of the documents. I was actually looking forward to making the trip again. I could enjoy the scenery even more knowing that everything would be approved. I had not gotten a picture of Mount Everest the previous day. Ankit assured me we would stop and get pictures. Wednesday I would be able to return to the legal office and pick up the paperwork.

When I got back to the hotel, Manisha and her father weren't there, so I went in search of another place to eat. Ankit thought it would be a good idea for all of us to be at the same place, so he made arrangements for Manisha and her father to relocate.

Later that afternoon, I was able to take Manisha out by myself for the first time. I carried her around on my hip as we walked the streets of Kathmandu looking through shop windows. There were lots of billboard advertisements for safaris through the jungle, elephant rides and plane trips into China, and escorted hiking trips by the Sherpas to Mount Everest.

Nepal has fourteen peaks more than twenty-six thousand feet high. In the Janakpur District alone, in the Mechi Zone of the Himalayas where we were, there were seven peaks more than fourteen thousand feet. The road on which we traveled gave us vistas of some of the highest peaks in the world with Mount Everest at 29,028 feet.

In a different time and place, I would have jumped at the

opportunity to go on one of the excursions. I had gone scuba diving all over the world, including diving with hundreds of Barracudas in the Bahamas. I bled blue blood when I was bit by a grouper at eighty feet on the Great Barrier Reef. I was waited on hand and foot and treated to spectacular diving in the Red Sea off the coast of Eilat, Israel, surrounded by poisonous lion fish and garden eel. I traveled to Europe more than once, studied in England and Italy, toured Australia and New Zealand, and chased sharks in the Caribbean.

I was in Jerusalem taking a course in Biblical Studies at the start of the 1991-1992 Gulf War. After being shown how to use a gas mask and self-administer a nerve gas antidote, I paid a hundred shekels in an all-night escape from Jerusalem to Tel Aviv. I caught the last plane out to Switzerland and then spent a few days in Engelberg skiing while the world was on the brink of war. I whitewater rafted down the Colorado River in the Grand Canyon and trekked through the rain forests of Central America in Belize and Honduras. I lived for myself, until God called me to adopt. Now it was as much fun to look at those advertisements with Manisha as it was to actually have experienced them a few years earlier.

I had become accustomed to the stares of the Nepali men which were more apparent to me now that Manisha was with me. I was stopped on the streets by shopkeepers, who spoke just enough English to sell trinkets to the tourists, "What caste is she?" they would ask, as if the higher the caste, the more value she had.

In Nepali society, the little girls did not have the same "worth" as young boys. Manisha's father wanted to remarry, which made him anxious to complete the adoption. He could not marry until the adoption was finalized or else Manisha would not meet the United States definition of orphan.

When Raj and his new wife had their own children, Manisha would have come after their children in hierarchy as far as food, clothing, and bare necessities. Her life at best would have been difficult and death was a certainty by the time she was seven.

After being asked several times, I thought I'd better find out. Ankit told me that Manisha was a Chetri, the second highest caste after Brahmin. Her last name in Nepali, Karki, was a common Chetri family name. It bothered me that everyone asked, but it was easier to answer the question than to evade it.

Many also thought Manisha was a boy because of her short, oily hair. When I later washed all the oil out, I was surprised that her hair was curly and thick. The substance her father kept lathering on her head prevented little critters from taking up residence. I later discovered lice. I relentlessly searched for the disgusting creatures on my new daughter's head while she squirmed impatiently—and was convinced the miniature, prehistoric-looking monsters were also on mine.

I couldn't wait to remove the nose ring and earrings. I had already come up with a plan for that. The red dot on the middle of her forehead also had to go.

I began to teach Manisha English and she made her first childish attempts to mimic the sounds I made—the word for lion, the word for flower, the word for cookie, the word for dirty, but her favorite word was "meow." Any cat we saw required at least a 30-second examination, maybe longer. She taught me the word "bani," which means rice, and Ankit made sure I knew the Nepali word for bathroom, which was Achi ayo.

We walked around for about an hour and a half, long enough to tire me out. Twenty-three pounds gets heavy after a while. As we headed back to the hotel, I heard another language being spoken that surprised me. A group of young people were talking in Hebrew. I turned around and asked if they were from Israel.

"Yes," they said. "We are on holiday." They described Nepal as a popular tourist spot for Israelis. Having studied Hebrew, I felt like I had met some new friends.

Upon arriving back at the Bleu, Ankit called about plans for the next day, "Don't worry about food, we'll stop and get something to eat."

That sounded good to me, or so I thought.

Chapter Eleven

...God has brought me laughter

Genesis 21:6

The next morning at 5:30 a.m. we were ready to go but Manisha and her father were not in the lobby. Ankit walked over and banged on their door to wake them up.

Shortly thereafter we took off in the van. The trip seemed to go faster this time, maybe because we had made it two days earlier. We drove for several hours and finally stopped.

"Let's eat here," Ankit said.

The building was dirty and dilapidated. Someone was out front cooking on the ground in a large steamy pot.

"The bathroom is downstairs," I was told as we entered inside the restaurant. I found the stairs and cautiously walked down. There were farm animals and chickens all over the place. The aroma smelled like a well-mixed concoction of manure and rice, with a little chicken seasoning thrown in. As I landed on the last step I looked straight ahead and realized there was no back to the building. If someone wasn't paying attention, they would walk off and fall into the river below. I wondered if Nepalis had ever heard of building codes.

I walked a few feet away from the stairs being careful not to step on any animals or something worse. There was a little room off to the right side. *Is that the bathroom,* I thought to myself? There was a bowl that appeared to contain water with chickens sitting all around it. Was that the toilet?

Maybe I was supposed to hang off the back of the building and sort of squat and hope to hit the river below. I didn't want to shoo the chickens away. I felt like asking, "Excuse me, chickens, could you please show me the bathroom or are you sitting on it? I don't want to ask the guys upstairs because they think I am a soft American girl."

I got nowhere with that idea. I decided to go back upstairs and just keep this little situation to myself. Bushes were preferable to fighting with chickens over their toilet.

By this time everybody had been served and was enjoying their meal. Whatever they were eating, it was very soupy. The "restaurant" was quite full and except for Ankit, everybody was eating with their hands. I looked at Manisha sitting with her father. They were also eating with their hands. I was totally disgusted and wondered if I would ever be able to westernize her.

"I'll just eat the rice and skip the other stuff," I told the cook. *A salad with ranch dressing would have been wonderful.* I picked up my bottled water, which I had gotten used to carrying with me, and took a sip. I felt fortunate that the restaurant had napkins. Nepalis didn't use napkins. When they were finished eating, they just wiped their hands on their clothes.

As I spooned my rice out of the dirty bowl, the rats scurrying around provided a new form of entertainment. I wondered how my life could have gotten so turned upside down.

Later in the day, as we continued on our journey, we stopped to take pictures of Mount Everest. What was it like to see the highest point on the face of the earth? I thought of Psalm 112:9, "He has scattered abroad His gifts to the poor…" It was difficult to pull myself away from admiring its grandeur, knowing I would probably never see it again.

As I looked at its tall, jagged snow-covered tops, I couldn't help but reflect on what precipice of danger might lay ahead of me. I felt like I was climbing my own Mount Everest. At least the mountain climbers and tourists brought in a measure of wealth and provided work for the Sherpas.

It wasn't long before we arrived at the CDO's office. As we waited for our turn, Ankit walked off to do something and I was left to myself. An old, pleasant man walked in and when he saw me waiting, he asked, "You speak English?"

"Yes, I do," I said. "I am an American."

His eyes lit up and he waved his hands like he wanted to

talk. He sat down beside me and started speaking in English. I had not met anyone in Nepal that spoke fluent English. He must have been in his 70's or 80's. To run into an old man in a remote region of Nepal who spoke almost perfect English—when half the population couldn't read or write—I didn't think that was possible.

He had enlisted in the British army in Nepal during World War II. Over 200,000 Nepalese men served in Gurkha battalions and fought on every front with heroic valor. Over 25,000 died in the war.

"I haven't spoken English in over fifty years," he told me. He cleared his throat, and once he got started, he didn't want to stop. For one day, he felt young again, as he reminisced about his service in the British army and spoke in a language he had almost forgotten.

I enjoyed listening to him. World War II had always piqued my interest and I love to hear people's stories. Who would have thought I would spend an afternoon in the remotest regions of Nepal listening to an old soldier recount his days from World War II? We all have stories to tell. I was glad I got to hear his.

Manisha and her father had stayed outside the building. They did not need to come into the CDO's office this time since the Officer had previously met them. Eventually Ankit returned and my name was called.

This time it was different. The CDO was excited to see us. He smiled and cordially invited us in. Today we were his guests and a male attendant brought us hot, spicy tea. I worried about the quality of the water, but wanting to follow proper etiquette, I took a sip. It was pretty tasty.

He continued to pour over the rest of my papers. He laughed at a comment by my boss. She said in my work reference I was a very talented person. I believe he read every single word.

At last he gathered up the papers and sent us downstairs to another area where we had to talk to someone else. The man rifled through the documents and seemed unable to find something.

Suddenly he asked, "Where is your home study?"

I had fortuitously made an extra copy and packed both along

with my six sets of other documents. If I had not made the second copy, they would not have been able to seal the first one. It would have meant going back to Kathmandu to make one copy of the Home Study, requiring a third trip over the mountains to Janakpur. As much as I enjoyed the beauty, I didn't want to make the trip a third time. Copy machines were a rare luxury here.

"I have it here," I told him. I quickly dug one copy out and handed it over. He took it and put it with all the other documents and sealed it.

I later told Ankit, "Nobody told me that I had to have six copies. If it hadn't been for the INS lady who Fed Ex'd it to me, I wouldn't have had even one."

Mission accomplished, we headed back to Kathmandu. It was late when we arrived and we decided to let Manisha stay with her father one more night. All of us would have to make a trip the next afternoon to the U.S. Embassy and more forms would have to be filled out. Afterwards Raj would be free to leave Kathmandu and go back to his village if he chose.

I felt conflicted as I thought about his departure. It made me happy to think Manisha would be all mine, but at the same time, it saddened me to think that she would never see her father again. I knew there would be tears of joy and tears of pain. How both could be true created a difficult and unsolvable paradox for me emotionally. When I reflected upon my own father leaving me at two years old and meeting him again when I turned thirty, I wondered, when that moment arrived for his departure, how I would feel.

Chapter Twelve

Let the little children come to me...

Matthew 19:14

The next day was Wednesday. Five days had passed since I had arrived in Kathmandu. We needed to return to the legal secretary's office to pick up more paperwork. As I met the government official, his unexplained hostility toward me felt like "...flaming arrows of the evil one" (Ephesians 6:16). His signature was required on one piece of paper. It wasn't like he had authority to not allow the adoption. He was sort of a "yes" man with ulterior motives.

I gave him my paperwork and then was required to sit in his office for a couple of hours. I sat bored and hungry as the time dragged by. When I was a court reporter waiting on attorneys and judges during trial proceedings, I would usually buy a chocolate candy bar out of one of the vending machines in the hallway. *How nice one would taste right now,* I thought, as my stomach growled.

"Do you have any candy around here," I asked the man?

He hunched down in his chair and looked at me with a stern look, "This is a very poor country." I got the message, but it wasn't my fault Nepal was poor and I was hungry. I was still an American living by American standards.

"You need these things copied again," he said.

I doubted that what he said was true. I had my six copies of everything. He made me wait two hours to tell me he needed another copy of something? I took my documents and we headed out to find a Xerox store nearby.

Manisha and I returned to his office an hour later.

"You will have to come back on Friday. Things aren't ready."

All he needed to do was sign the document, but there was nothing I could do. We left the Home Ministry office and headed back to the hotel. Later that afternoon, we also had to visit the U.S. Embassy so Raj could fill out his portion of the documents.

Between filling out tedious documents and dealing with cranky bureaucrats, Manisha and I had time to get to know each other. Meal times were especially entertaining. I took her out for the first time to eat on Wednesday. The waiter brought us a Coke and a couple of straws. I sipped out of my mine and Manisha tried to sip out of hers. She had watched me use one and then spent the whole time in Nepal trying to imitate me. I gave her a fork and a spoon to use instead of her hands, but she found the utensils more fun to play with and still preferred eating with her hands.

There were no high chairs or booster seats in the restaurants and sitting at a table to eat was a new thing. She thought it was fun to go up and down and move the chair around, much to the chagrin of people sitting around us. Once she fell backwards and I almost panicked. I had my first taste of motherly guilt.

Manisha was fascinated with my long blonde hair and loved to stroke it. She was also interested in touching my face, which I presumed was an intimate way of getting to know me, and as she ran her hand over my facial features, I would name what they were—eyes, ears, nose, and mouth—as a game until she learned all the parts.

Toilets were a continual source of entertainment. She loved to watch anything thrown in disappear. I had to be careful to monitor what she discarded. She loved to brush her teeth but didn't know to spit the toothpaste back into the sink. Her spit would land on the floor. I had to teach her that trash gets put in the trash can, panties are worn underneath outerwear, little girls sleep in a nightgown, and I used Vaseline on my lips at night to keep them moist.

I woke up one morning to find she had covered everything in Vaseline—my suitcase, my purse, the vanity beside my bed. I spent the next week uncovering various places where Vaseline had found its mark.

The television in the waiting area of the hotel captivated Manisha from the moment she laid eyes on it. It didn't matter that it was in black and white and boring. It was new to her and a big toy.

As I reflect fourteen years later, I am amused at the little things she found so interesting and entertaining. Her world in the remote mountains of Nepal was so small compared to the world she was witnessing for the first time even before we left Kathmandu.

Wednesday afternoon after lunch I took Manisha and her father out for a little shopping. Raj needed some new clothes and books for his school work. Most of the clothes I had brought Manisha from the States were too big, and she needed new shoes. This was one of those special moments I had waited for a long time.

We found a store and the salesperson handed us a brand-new pair of shoes and matching socks. Until now Manisha had never seen socks. When she realized the presents were for her, she quickly tossed the old shoes aside and eagerly put on the new ones. Her life was being transformed one step at a time. She walked out of the shoe store determinedly putting one foot in front of the other.

"These are my new shoes my mommy bought me," she told anyone that would listen. She stopped people on the street to tell them about her new shoes.

I had much to learn from my little one, who had such an innocent trust in accepting what she couldn't fully understand. She wanted the world to know she had new shoes and that was all that mattered.

After we finished our shopping we headed back to the Bleu Hotel. I took some instant pictures with a Polaroid camera that I gave to Manisha's father. The pictures I wanted to keep I took with my Nikon camera.

There was sadness in my heart because Manisha's father would be leaving. These moments in the hotel lobby marked the last ones Manisha would spend with him. Would God be sufficient as I would feel her pain, her anger, her tears, and her terror?

The door was closing on the world she had known. She had to say good-bye to her old life to receive her new one. She would have to grieve her loss, but a new inheritance in Christ awaited her. God wanted to give her something better—a chance to dream, to feel a mother's love, and to know her heavenly Father.

We took a few more pictures and her father said good-bye before heading to his hotel room. Manisha was preoccupied with examining the pictures and didn't notice that he had left. Unfortunately he came back out into the lobby. He thought he had forgotten something, but he hadn't, and then proceeded back to his room.

Manisha tried to follow after him. She ran down the hallway, but he shut the door before she got there. I was a few feet behind and caught up to her. She was crying and banging on the door calling for him in Nepali. I tried to pick her up, but she pulled away. I waited to see if her father opened the door one more time but he never did. Manisha cried hysterically.

I was crying on the inside because I had so much love to give her but she couldn't receive it. All she wanted was him. I picked her up and carried her up the four flights of stairs, her cries echoing down the stairway. I set her down on the bed and locked the door so she couldn't leave.

Digging around in my suitcase to find something to distract her with, I pulled out some Play-Doh and rolled it around in my hand making various shapes. After several minutes she started paying more attention to that and less to the door. We sat together playing, not saying a word. Her big, brown eyes were captivated with the rolled snake shapes that I made into a necklace and bracelet. As she continued to be intrigued with the Play-Doh, I had some rice brought up to the room so we didn't have to leave.

Later in the evening I went in to shower before heading to bed. Manisha didn't want to bathe or put her nightgown on so I let her be. When I came out of the shower, I saw a poor little girl who stood beside her bed with her head lying on the pillow fast asleep.

Even though I knew I was in God's will, it didn't mean things would be easy. The hardest, most painful part of Manisha's adoption was I couldn't take away her loss. I had also suffered the same thirty-six years earlier, but in His Word, God promised to take care of orphans and widows (Jas 1:27). I clung to that knowing someday God would receive the "weight of glory."

Chapter Thirteen

…Am I My Brother's Keeper

Genesis 4:19

Fortunately in life there can only be one first. The first night Manisha spent with me away from her father was the hardest. The next day was chalked full of things to do, including a check-up at the doctor's, a T.B test, and an American Visa to allow Manisha to come to America. Ankit accompanied me on all of these errands because I had no idea where to go.

In the afternoon after running errands, we would return to the Bleu for a few hours to give Manisha a short nap. It wasn't so much I wanted her to nap as I wanted to rid her of those nasty nose and ear rings.

For three days when she was fast asleep, beginning with the nose ring, I cut the string and yanked it out. I felt like a fisherman with a catch ensnared by a lure. Each time she woke up screaming knowing something had happened but not knowing what. By the fourth day she refused to take the nap, but the Hindu symbols were gone and she looked like an American girl.

I had not found a decent place to eat so I decided to go upscale to the Mount Everest Hotel. I was still thinking about a salad with ranch dressing. The Mount Everest was a Five-Star Western Hotel and I was pleasantly surprised to find beef on the menu. I ordered my salad and got Manisha the biggest hamburger I had ever seen.

We were seated in a lavishly decorated dining room and treated to superb service that made me feel important. I lamented how I wished I could afford to stay there. My fourth floor flat at the Bleu, with no air-conditioning in the hot, humid Nepali air, was a far cry from this place. I wasn't sure if it was the beauty that made it so appealing or the familiarity with Western cuisine. By this time I was having pangs of homesickness and it looked like "home."

After eating we went to check out the swimming pool and I imagined how much fun it would be for the two of us. Manisha's eyes bulged as she stared at the water. We would later return for a visit to the "bathtub" when we had more time.

The next day on Friday, we needed to go back to the legal secretary's office to pick up the signed paperwork. When we arrived, however, much to my chagrin, nothing had been done. The legal secretary was playing games with me. He kept telling me that I would not be able to adopt Manisha because there was a problem with my paperwork.

However, when I refused to "buy" into his version of things, his demeanor abruptly changed.

"Here is my phone, call me," and the legal secretary put a small piece of paper in my hand and clasped my fingers over it. He either wanted money or sexual favors. I wasn't sure which.

I sat there for hours with Manisha, bored, watching other adoptive couples pass through while he refused to process us. A Japanese couple came in with a little boy in a knapsack on the back of his mother.

He said, "Their baby is going to grow up Japanese. Your baby is going to grow up American."

I sometimes think about the little boy with his new Japanese mother and father. We were like ships in the night passing each other—two children from a poor country adopted into different cultures presented before a man who thought more of himself than he ought. I have wondered, though saved from a life of poverty and hopelessness, if he would ever come to know the real Hope Giver.

The legal secretary said to me, "Your paperwork won't be ready until tomorrow." It was difficult for me not to be angry. I gathered Manisha and my things and left.

Later that afternoon I took Manisha back to the Everest Hotel to go swimming, but she was fearful of the water. Only the tops of her feet made it in the cold, spring-like pool. She wouldn't let me swim either. I had to settle for enjoying the pool from a distance.

We spent a couple of quiet, peaceful hours relaxing. Manisha thought my purse was full of interesting things and loved dumping out the contents. She drew doodles in a little book of quotes for new mothers I had stashed away. Her little scribbles I later called my first "love notes."

My daughter now had a mother as a role model and she wasted no time in learning all about "girlie" things. When she discovered my makeup, she insisted on trying it out. She smacked the lip gloss on her lips, but found it more fun to smear it on her cheeks. The eyeliner gave her a "black eye," but she fluttered her eyes anyway as if she were beautiful. She also tried out my sunglasses, taking them off of me, putting them on herself, and then putting them back on me.

The noisy environment of Kathmandu faded into the distance as I enjoyed the peacefulness of the Everest Hotel. The Bleu was located in the heart of downtown Kathmandu. It was a maze of people, bikes, motorcycles, cows, and taxies. I had seen more dung than anyone would care to see in a lifetime. One little dog sitting in the street covered with fleas and mange reminded me of my dog Gypsy. He was pathetic and sad. I wished I could have helped him.

On one occasion I got lost in the wrong place, ending up at the local meat market. Before I could turn away to avoid the gore, I saw bodies of dogs sliced in half dangling from ropes waiting to be sold for food. Goat heads stared back at me. The stench was nauseatingly gruesome with bright red blood covering the street. I tripped over people trying to avoid stepping in it. I supposed the trash trucks came by sometimes but not often enough.

At the Everest Hotel, I tried to put things I didn't want to remember in the back of my mind. Manisha and I could be alone without reminders of her father, particularly the door to his motel room that continued to cause anxiety.

I wanted to escape from the culture around me but I couldn't. In America I could change the television dial if something made me uncomfortable. I could ignore the starving children, the murders, and the rapes.

"Am I my brother's keeper?" Cain asked God.

I can hear the indifference to God about his brother in Cain's reply. I didn't want to be like Cain, but Nepal forced me to confront what was in my heart and I didn't like what I saw.

Friday night, as I put Manisha to bed, we looked through a magazine that I had brought from the States. It had lots of pictures of dogs and cats, and I pointed to a cat and went "meow," as I had done all week. She was intrigued with the kittens and said her first American word that wasn't just imitating my English sounds, but where she knew what it meant—an almost perfect "meow."

I scooted beside her in bed as she looked at me with her big brown eyes. I had no idea what she was thinking, but I could tell she was thinking pretty deep thoughts. Spontaneously she let out a big smile that melted my heart and I gave her a huge bear hug.

Love has a way of conquering all. My worries for today, my fears for tomorrow, any mistakes I'd made in the past, and my sinfulness that would scar the image of God within me if it were possible—swallowed up in victory. God's redemptive love turned my tears into joy. I couldn't wait until we were "home."

Chapter Fourteen

...when I am weak, then I am strong

II Corinthians 12:10

Saturday arrived making it one week I had been in Nepal. Today would be the first time we went to church together.

A taxi dropped us off nearby, but I had forgotten where the building was. After much walking around in circles, somebody noticed us.

"Are you looking for something?" A man asked.

"I am looking for the Christian Church," I told him.

He showed me where it was and I thanked him. Could he have been an angel in disguise? I was surprised he spoke English.

After leaving our shoes at the door, Manisha and I walked in and sat down on the floor among the women.

"Namaste," I greeted them with, the traditional hello in Nepali. Several ladies smiled at me and spoke to Manisha in her language. I had looked forward to the sermon but today it was delivered in Nepali so I didn't understand the message. I bided the time keeping Manisha quiet, which wasn't hard to do. Uncharacteristically, I felt tired.

We had been invited for lunch after the service by the Reeses, so we hitched a ride on the back of the bikes of their children. As we were riding over to their home, Manisha told Doug Reese about her new shoes. Everyone she met got an earful about them as she was not shy.

After stepping through their front door I felt like I had been transported back to America. A taste of familiarity to a homesick traveler is like sweet apple pie and vanilla ice cream to a starving soul. Their home seemed like a palace compared to what I had seen of Nepal. Debby Reese kept busy as a doctor and Doug was active working with the students at the University of Kathmandu. They were affiliated with one of the organizations on campus and had been in Nepal for several years.

A wonderfully delicious lunch was prepared that hit my sweet spot. Earlier in the week I had been craving a nice cold glass of milk. Ice trucks would make a daily appearance in front of the Bleu, loaded with milk and other things I didn't recognize. One day I purchased a small carton, and after swallowing several gulps, I realized the milk had already soured. I gagged and held my nose to keep from throwing up. Even orange juice did not taste like orange juice. The bananas appeared oddly too small— only eggs seemed to look like eggs. I supposed chickens were the same everywhere.

The Reeses had done what they had promised—treated me to a real American meal. We had ice tea, salad, chicken, beans and dessert that resembled ordinary food back home.

For the first time in a week I was able to enjoy speaking English, at least using a few more words than dirty, cookie, and meow.

When I asked to use their facilities, they hollered to me as I walked down the hall, "There is toilet paper."

I laughed. Ankit must have told them some things when I left the table.

I enjoyed the lunch except I felt very tired. We left about 4:00 in the afternoon and headed back. A short time later I began to feel worse. After putting Manisha down early, I went to bed about 10:00 feeling like I had just come off the scream machine at Six Flags Over Georgia.

I started thinking back to what I had eaten. Maybe it was the salad at the Everest Hotel. Could it have been the rice I ate on the way to Janakpur? How about rat feces?

Manisha had chronic diarrhea so I thought I may have caught something from her. Every day I awakened to the ritual of people making unspeakable noises in the early morning hours. I tried not to be so loud.

After several hours of misery, I called down to the lobby and asked if I could have a doctor come see me. The night attendant had someone sent up to my room. Manisha was still asleep.

"You…stay in bed…take…pills … I write prescriptions," he said.

He handed me several pieces of paper containing illegible writing. Speaking in broken English, I didn't understand half of what he said, and I did not know where to obtain the pills. I called down to the lobby again.

"I send runner out in morning when it's light to get pills," the man said.

A while later an errand boy knocked on my door. I gave him a tip but apparently it wasn't enough. He didn't seem happy but I was too sick to try to find more in my disorderly purse.

Manisha was awake and I wondered how I would take care of her. She called for her father since I did not respond as usual. For the next couple of hours I got lots of exercise running back and forth between the bed and the toilet.

I needed a better plan. I phoned the Reeses to see if they could take care of Manisha while I went to the legal office to check on my paperwork. I didn't have enough strength to take her with me, and I needed to get the paperwork completed because it was delaying everything else.

I had no plans to spend the day staring at the ceiling or reading on the throne. I threw the pills away so Manisha wouldn't find them. The Reeses were happy to take Manisha. We made a plan that seemed simple enough, but then nothing in Nepal was simple. I would take a taxi to a school, call them from the school, and they would pick her up. The taxi would take me to the legal office.

The front desk called a cab. Since the driver spoke no English, the clerk told him where I wanted to go, but he didn't explain everything to him.

He needed to wait for me in front of the school while I made the phone call. After Manisha was picked up, he would take me to the legal office. To make sure I wasn't stranded, I didn't pay him. I could hear him yelling loudly at me as I exited the taxi and briskly walked up to the school with Manisha in tow.

I asked if I could use their phone but the woman said, "No, you can't use the phone."

Why not? Nobody was talking on it. I felt too sick to argue with the woman.

I walked out of the door in tears, crying to God, "Please help me."

I could hear her locking the door behind me.

About that time, another lady walked up and asked in English, "What is wrong?"

"I need to use the phone but the woman inside won't let me."

"Come in and I'll let you use it," she said kindly. She unlocked the door and let me in. She took us over to the phone and handed it to me. I called the Reeses.

The conversation took only a minute as they were waiting for my call. When I turned to thank the mysterious figure that had let me in, she was gone. I looked around the school lobby and out front but she was nowhere to be found. It was the second time I wondered if I had met an angel in disguise.

The Reeses showed up a few minutes later and the taxi driver, still waiting for his money, followed them to their apartment. They took Manisha and she started to cry. I felt badly leaving her.

I had the taxi driver—for once I was glad I didn't speak Nepali—take me to the legal office. Upon arriving, I gave the poor, confused guy a nice sum of money for his trouble. I am sure he thought *good riddance.*

I walked into the legal office and plopped down in front of the official, making no effort about my appearance.

"What's wrong with you?" He asked.

"I am sick."

He could have cared less.

I thought, *maybe I will puke on you and then you will give me my papers.*

I didn't have a Christ-like attitude, but I was sick and didn't want to have an accident and bring humiliation on myself.

After a couple of hours, he got tired of looking at me. He left and came back later.

"You can go into this other room and wait."

He directed me to a dark room and I sat for another hour and waited. He probably put me there because he didn't want to look at me. After another hour, he told me to go see another man and he would have all of my papers. I went into another room and faced another man. He glanced through my documents.

"Everything is in order." He said.

After stamping them, he handed them to me. After all the waiting, it took five minutes. I thanked him and left.

I managed to get out of the building and took a few steps away from the pedestrian walkway before collapsing on the ground. I tried to be discreet about my situation as people walked by.

At least the Nepali side of the adoption was done. I wouldn't have to deal with the legal office anymore. I just had to give the U.S. Embassy proof that everything was legal so they would issue Manisha a U.S. passport.

I got a taxi back to the Bleu and called the Reeses so they could return Manisha. Shortly they arrived, and although I was feeling awful, I refused to let them keep her for the night.

"I can't do that to her," I told them, "no matter how badly I feel." I tucked Manisha into bed early again and collapsed on the bed. The phone rang about 9:00 p.m. and the light displayed it was the front desk.

"Manisha's father is here in the lobby and he wants to see Manisha."

I wondered what he was doing in Kathmandu. I thought he had returned to his village.

I politely told the attendant, feeling guilty, "Tell him he can come tomorrow. I am sick and can't come down tonight."

I overheard him speaking in Nepali to Manisha's father.

He came back on the phone, "He says it's okay."

I was relieved and hung up. Manisha had seemed exceptionally quiet since returning from the Reeses. I saw confusion in her eyes.

The next morning when I woke up, I realized I could hardly move. I willed myself to get us dressed and walked downstairs to meet Ankit and Alisha in the lobby. They had come over to finish the paperwork.

"Are you okay?" Ankit asked me.

Handing me a piece of paper to fill out, I started filling in the blanks and realized I couldn't read the questions.

Ankit grabbed them from me. "I'm taking you to the hospital."

Alisha took Manisha, and fortunately, she didn't protest this time.

We walked a couple of streets over to the Himalayan Clinic run for Westerners who frequently get sick. The clinic had just opened for business. We walked in and I slumped down in a chair. Ankit spoke to the receptionist in Nepali.

After a few minutes they took me to the back. Ankit asked me if I wanted him to come or wait in the lobby. I wanted him to translate.

Fortunately the doctor and nurse spoke English fairly well. The doctor poked on my belly and said, "You need fluids. You are very dehydrated. People die here all the time from dehydration. You are very sick."

The nurse took me into another room and hooked me up to an I.V. I was relieved to see that it looked like an American clinic. It appeared sanitary and reassured me I wouldn't die in a dirty Nepali hospital. Ankit had told me stories about the medical care and it sent shivers down my spine.

As the hours passed and the intravenous fluids coursed through my veins, I began to feel better. I relaxed on the cot from 9:00 in the morning until 4:00 in the afternoon with six bottles of I.V. fluid being pumped into me.

Ankit later returned to check on me. "How are you feeling?" he asked.

"Much better."

"You need to come with me to one place," he said. "You have to sign something I can't sign for you." He had spent the day trying to finish paperwork so I could return home. The doctor disconnected me from the I.V. and I felt strong enough to accompany Ankit.

We took a taxi to a government office where I signed one document and then he brought me back to the hotel. We decided it would be better for Manisha to stay with Ankit and his wife for the night to give me more time to recuperate.

After Ankit dropped me off, I began to feel sick again. I

headed back over to the Himalayan Clinic before it closed. The nurse gave me another shot of something to ease the nausea and I left hoping I would feel better.

Back at the hotel I tried not to be anxious, relaxing in bed and sipping small amounts of water, but I couldn't keep it down. I was getting better but not fast enough. Patience had never been my greatest virtue. Considering how close I came to dying from Cholera, I needed to be thankful I was alive. How dreadful it would have been had Manisha lost two mothers from the same disease.

The next morning, although I felt weak, I did not feel sick. I wanted American food to soothe my achy stomach.

I called the Reeses and asked them if there was a Western-style grocery store close by. I couldn't handle the local food market anymore. I knew the sights and smells would trigger a return of the nausea from the previous day.

They told me about a little grocery store down the street for trekkers and hikers. I left the hotel and headed in what I thought was the right direction and found it. I wondered why I couldn't have found the place a week ago. I got exactly what I wanted— Saltine crackers.

I munched on the crackers and began to feel better than I had felt in a couple of days. Ankit called and asked if I felt well enough to take Manisha.

I couldn't wait to get her back. He and Alisha showed up in a little bit to drop her off, but Manisha was angry and would not come to me. I was disappointed but understood her reaction. In some ways we would have to start over again.

Only a few things remained to be done before we could leave. I had to pick up Manisha's Visa at the U.S. Embassy. We went there first. Manisha fought with me the whole time and screamed loudly for her father. Her outburst worried me that the Embassy might not grant me her Visa, but they didn't pay her any attention.

After a longer wait than expected, they handed me the precious document. From there we headed over to the Thai Airlines to get my ticket changed from May 16th to May 6th. The only way to do it was to spend two nights in Bangkok.

"Can you put us in a nice hotel?" I asked the ticket agent.

"Do you have a Visa for your daughter?"

"Yes."

He was asking about a Thai Visa, but I was referring to the American Visa. I would later wish that, "A rose by any other name would smell as sweet." [3]

I left the Thai ticket office and headed back. I decided to check us out of the Bleu Hotel and stay at the Everest Hotel for one night. Things were going dreadfully between us. I wanted to be in a different environment for Manisha with nothing to remind her of her father or my sickness; and to start afresh in a place that was more in keeping with a soft American girl.

I quickly packed everything and a waiting taxi took us to the hotel. It was also close to the airport and more convenient. After checking in we had some time in the afternoon to relax by the pool. I coaxed Manisha into the water up to her legs.

After swimming we went back up to our hotel room to get ready for a special evening. I gave Manisha a hot, bubbly bath and washed her hair. As I showered she watched a television broadcast from the States starring Barney, the purple dinosaur. She sat on the bed and clapped to the tune of, "I love you, you love me, we're a happy family…" Later that became her favorite television show. Sweet memories. I almost felt like Manisha liked Barney more than me but at least she was mine.

We didn't have a brown-out while she took her bath, but we did when I took my shower. Many of my experiences in Nepal had to do with bathrooms and toilets and bodily fluids. This time I was taking a shower when the power went out. I couldn't remember how to turn the water off, how to open the shower door, or where my towel was. It was quite a new experience to be lost in a totally dark bathroom. Brown-outs were quite common and this was a "gotcha" one.

Alisha and Ankit arrived later in the evening and I treated them to a tasty meal. Ankit mentioned that Manisha's father had called wanting to see her one more time. I suggested he come by the hotel after 10:00 that night when she would be asleep.

---

[3] Shakespeare's *Romeo and Juliet*, 1594

As we sat in the dining room feasting together, I reflected on my time in Nepal, how God had made everything possible even when things seemed impossible. We shared stories, reveling in God's blessings. Manisha fell asleep in my arms and I took her up to the room to tuck her into bed. Raj, her father, stopped by and said a sweet goodbye to me in the lobby without seeing Manisha one last time.

The next day the world changed.

Chapter Fifteen

...I will bring your children from the east

Isaiah 43:5

I was awakened by the phone ringing before daylight. It was Ankit.

"The communists are striking today," he said. "Nobody is supposed to travel on the roads because it's dangerous. Everything is closed. I am not even sure we can make it to see you off."

It wouldn't make any difference as far as Manisha and I getting to the airport. We were just a couple of miles away. I was glad we had checked out of the Bleu which was near the epicenter of the political turmoil. I would have been disappointed if they had not shown up, but they made it.

After checking in our bags and sharing hugs, Manisha and I stood in line to board the plane, waving goodbye. I handed the attendant my passport, Manisha's official travel document, and our airline tickets.

The Thai attendant looked at my paperwork. My heart skipped a beat as I could see in his expression that something was wrong.

"You can get on the plane, but she can't." He said. "She doesn't have a Thai Visa with her documents."

Ankit came over to see what was wrong. We looked at each other not knowing what he was talking about. We had not been told that any Thai Visa would be needed. There must have been some mistake.

Passengers continued to board the plane as the Thai official pulled us out from the line. He suggested we talk to somebody with more authority. Maybe a higher-up person could explain to us the problem. We were escorted to a private room to talk with a supervisor.

"You can get on the plane," he said. "You don't need a Thai passport because you have an American passport, but your Nepali daughter does not have an American passport. She has to have a Thai passport to stay for more than twenty-four hours in Thailand."

I tried to explain to him that we had to stay two nights in Bangkok to make the travel connections work.

"Manisha can't stay more than twenty-four hours in Thailand," the Thai official said again.

Despite my protests and pleas, including being willing to sit in jail while waiting, they weren't going to bend the rules.

"Why don't you go to the Thai Embassy quickly and get one," the supervisor suggested.

That was easier said than done. It was a long ways from the airport. Ankit wasn't sure with the strike if we could even travel on the roads. The Maoists, who had instituted the strike, had roadblocks set up throughout Kathmandu.

"They could throw stones at us. It's very dangerous," Ankit cautioned. I could tell Alisha did not want us to go. On a motorcycle we would be easy targets. I wasn't deterred. I wanted to try.

I gave Manisha a hug and handed her to Alisha. Ankit and I walked out of the airport and I followed him to his motorcycle feeling guilty for putting both of us in danger.

I didn't know which was scarier: Speeding on a motorcycle or Communists stoning us with rocks.

I hoped we could do it quickly and get back before the plane left. On the motorcycle we were able to go around the blockades. I thanked God as we passed each one without incident. We finally arrived at the Thai Embassy but there were no cars in the parking lot. We got off the motorcycle and walked up to the closed door. On the door hung a hastily-written sign.

Ankit translated for me. "Closed today." There was nothing we could do to get a Thai passport for Manisha until they reopened. With the political situation it was hard to know when that would be.

Feeling totally deflated, we went back to the airport. I tried to plead my case again with the Thai officials.

"The Embassy is closed because of the strike and I can't get the passport," I pleaded. "Please let Manisha on the plane. I was sick and almost died, and I am out of money and I need to get home." My tears of persuasion got me nowhere. They refused to listen.

Ankit explained. "They are Thai, not Nepali. They are different. They are not going to be flexible about the rules like Nepali."

My flight had already left so I had to change my plane ticket. I didn't know to what. I returned to the ticket agent to see what was available hoping to get the passport the next day. All the flights were booked until May 16. I couldn't imagine being stuck in Kathmandu for ten days. It would be hard getting by on just a credit card. I wasn't sure I could obtain more cash.

"We have available first class tickets for both of you for $3,500 and you can go home in two days," The attendant said.

"Three thousand five hundred dollars, did you say?" I stared at him in disbelief. I didn't have that kind of money. There was only one thing left to do. We retrieved our suitcases and went back to the Everest Hotel.

We arrived to find Alisha and Manisha in the restaurant eating rice. I lugged our belongings back up to the room, and as I walked in the phone rang. The Thai ticket agent was on the line. He had gotten permission for us to board the flight that left on Friday—two days from now.

"The flight is overbooked by two hundred people, but I was able to get special permission," he said.

I humbly thanked him. As I put the phone down, I wondered how he was able to reach me. I had not told him where I was staying.

I sat on the bed feeling numbed by the turn of events, thanking God for his mercy. I wanted to go home. I couldn't believe God made it happen without paying $3,500.

Indeed, as I have written it, and as the terrified disciples spoke of Jesus when He rebuked the waves, "Who is this? Even the wind and the waves obey Him (Mark 5:41)!'"

> Now to Him who is able to do immeasurably more than all we ask or imagine, according to His power that is at work within us, to Him be glory in the church and in Jesus Christ throughout all generations, forever and ever! Amen (Ephesians 3:20-21).

——— ———

Fourteen years later, as I hold my Zirconium and sterling silver necklace up in the bright Florida sunshine, it sparkles with the same radiance as when I bought it for a few rupees in Nepal the following day. Manisha also has a necklace that was thrown in the bag with mine as a free gift. It's her favorite necklace. I wonder if the best things in life are free.

They are our only keepsakes from Nepal as I did no shopping for souvenirs. I realize now I needed them because they help me to remember my struggle and ultimate victory while in Nepal. They are tangible reminders of God's faithfulness and mercy in the severest of circumstances.

By the next day, the Maoists had abandoned their efforts to bring about a revolution and life returned to normal. Political climates change quickly in developing nations. We no longer needed a Thai passport for Manisha and spent the day shopping and basking in the sun beside the pool.

God had restored what was lost. For the first time since my arrival, I had peace and Manisha was content. We made a visit to a local park and took pictures of the beautiful Nepali flowers.

I handed my camera to a man standing nearby and showed him what I wanted him to do. Several other men walked over and wanted to look through the lens. I don't think they had ever seen a camera before. I eventually got him to snap a couple of pictures of us that hopefully would turn out.

Later I discovered all the pictures were cocked sideways since he didn't know what he was doing. It's funny the things that stay with us and the things we forget. I hadn't thought about that for a long time.

It was a skewed picture through which I had viewed God. God didn't always give me what I wanted. He gave me what I needed. I had no idea how special the day would be. I could only see through a lens of wanting to be home, but God in His infinite wisdom saw through a heavenly lens. He wanted me to have pictures of beauty, peace, happiness, hope and enchantment, if for no other reason than to reveal God's redemptive love. Dealing with documents, worry, fear, travel, bureaucrats, propositions, sickness, tears, blockades, and exhaustion were now a thing of the past.

On Friday morning, Ankit came to the Everest Hotel to see us off but did not accompany us to the airport. We said our goodbyes not knowing when we would see each other again. Such a man of God with a servant's heart, I bid him farewell on his journey to carry the Gospel to the uttermost regions of Nepal. Hopefully through Manisha's adoption, God had inspired him with a renewed zeal to give orphaned children not only hope but a chance to know the Real Hope Giver.

Following a six-hour wait for the plane in the airport lounge, we walked out onto the tarmac to board. Manisha stared wide-eyed as the baggage handlers loaded the suitcases into the belly of the plane. The roar from the engines was deafening. She clasped my pants leg for security and protection from the wind. The mountains, the cows, the rundown buildings, the tattered Nepali signs that were my first impressions of Nepal when I arrived two weeks earlier filled me with nostalgia. We were going home.

We found our seats and settled in for the long trip. Our flight arrived in Bangkok, Thailand around midnight. We stayed overnight in a hotel inside the airport, and left early the next morning for the flight to Los Angeles. Upon arriving at the Los Angeles International Airport, my heart quickened. We were almost home.

Because Manisha was not an American citizen, we had to go through the section of the airport designated for people emigrating from other countries. We waited in a long line and watched as families stood before the U.S. Immigration and Customs Officer and were cleared to leave. A family with two young boys was next.

The Immigrations official called them up. He checked each of their papers and stamped them.

"Welcome to America," He said.

"Thank you," they answered. They grabbed their few belongings as in a daze and made their way to the exit. I wondered if that was all they owned, the few small suitcases they pulled behind them. I hoped America would be everything they dreamed of.

It was now our turn. I stepped up and handed the Immigrations Agent my passport and Manisha's travel document.

After glancing at my papers, he stamped them and said, "Welcome to America."

We were home. Almost.

We stayed overnight in the Los Angeles Marriot near the airport and arrived at the Atlanta Hartsfield International Airport the following day. We were greeted by my mother; my sister, Paige; Paula, my long-time friend from childhood; her husband, and two children. Mother arrived with an armful of clothes and we shared a special moment as she admired her first grandchild.

While I was in Nepal I had prayed that God would protect my dad from taking a turn for the worse until I arrived home. The brain tumor diagnosed the previous year had impaired him to where it would have been too hard for him to come, and it saddened me that he was unable to meet us. He would have been so proud of his new granddaughter, but where God closes a door He opens a window. His illness had been one of the things God used to give me the vision and strength to pursue my dreams. He lived long enough to meet Manisha before passing away a few months later.

It was May 8, 1994, Mother's Day. After visiting for a couple of hours at the airport terminal in Atlanta, we boarded the plane for the final leg of our trip. At 6:00 p.m., Sunday night, we landed in Gainesville, Florida. Manisha had fallen asleep and I carried her down the steps of the plane and walked across the tarmac to the airport entrance. As I walked in with Manisha in my arms, we were greeted by friends and my One Another Group. It was a wonderful "welcome home" party, not unlike the day when we will arrive at our "eternal home." Jed Keesling, one of the church elders, gathered us around in the parking lot and prayed for our future. God had answered the prayers of the saints to bring Manisha home. I felt blessed to call them my friends.

Manisha's adoption showed me that the Kingdom of Heaven was at hand. My treasure from God, hidden in the mountains of Nepal, was not unlike the man in Matthew 13:44, who found a treasure hidden in a field, and sold all he had and bought the field. The journey of a thousand miles had only just begun. Another adoption lay in the future. There were mountains to climb and valleys to cross.

...yet not my will, but yours be done
(Luke 22:42).

Chapter Sixteen

Cast your bread upon the waters...

Ecclesiastes 11:1

In C.S. Lewis' book, *Prince Caspian*, when Lucy told Aslan "I thought you'd come roaring in and frighten all the enemies away," Aslan told her, "...things never happen the same way twice." That could be said of my journey.

I knew from the beginning I wanted two children. After seeing how God worked in Manisha's adoption, the miracles and answered prayers, I assumed the second one would go much the same way. It didn't. When things happened the first time, I was changed by them. When I started the second adoption, I wasn't the same person I was when I adopted Manisha.

The world never remains the same either. Countries change adoption requirements. Some countries close adoption programs while new ones open.

Our thoughts are way too limited to begin to comprehend what God might be doing. Isaiah 55:8 says, "For my thoughts are not your thoughts, neither are your ways my ways, declares the Lord." I had no idea how different things would be the second time around. I am glad I didn't know.

When Manisha was five, I began to talk with her about adopting "a little baby sister." She was excited and couldn't wait to have a "playmate." I am not sure she understood it all, but it was the beginning of a long process to prepare her for a new arrival.

I wanted to adopt again from Nepal, but Nepal only allowed families to adopt one boy and one girl. I wanted another little girl. I also wanted to use the same adoption agency. The only country the adoption agency was licensed to work with that met my criteria of a single mother with one daughter was Vietnam.

Vietnam was expensive. I spent a lot of time counting the cost financially. Could I afford it? Did I have the energy to raise a second child? Could I give two children what they needed emotionally, physically, mentally, academically and spiritually?

With the Lord helping me, I thought I could do all those things. I didn't want to be so fearful that my fear prevented me from taking the risk. I was stepping out in faith that God would provide.

In the spring of 1997, I contacted the adoption agency and began the process of filling out forms. I bought a book on Vietnam published by the same company that produced the book I had bought on Nepal. I began to tell people, "I am adopting again, this time from Vietnam."

I was surprised that things were not the same this time around. I didn't have the support from my family or friends. I got comments like, "Don't you think being a single parent to one child is enough? How are you going to handle a second child?" All the comments came from well-meaning Christians, but nevertheless, they were negative and discouraging.

If Manisha had been struggling in school, I would have given all of my attention to helping her and not pursued a second adoption. Since she was three when she arrived here, she would have been considered at-risk for developmental and mental delays.

Health problems would also have been a red flag, but Manisha had never been sick with more than just a runny nose or fever and I hadn't missed a day of work since arriving home from Nepal.

One weekend, my church had a women's retreat, and though I'm not much of a retreat person, I decided to go. I wanted to be alone with God to pray earnestly about my plans for a second adoption. I left Manisha with the Murphys for the long weekend and drove with some friends to Daytona Beach, Florida.

I sought solace and prayed fervently asking God to show me His will. One evening I took a stroll along the beach, and I said, "Lord, if I find the perfect conch shell, I will take that as a sign that you are leading me in this direction."

I didn't find just one conch shell, I found many conch shells. I quit counting them after a while. They were all perfectly formed baby shells. I picked up one that was particularly beautiful and squeezed it in my hand.

"Thank you, Lord, for giving me this sign."

The next day, Sunday, as we gathered in the restaurant for lunch before heading back to Gainesville, there was a raffle. The first prize was a beautifully handmade baby scrapbook.

I said, "God, if you want me to adopt another child, please let me win this as another sign." There were at least sixty women in the room. I won it. As I walked up to receive my prize, I had goose bumps. I knew God was speaking to me.

However, during the next three years as I experienced the darkest hours of my Christian life, no pictures adorned its blank pages. I wondered if I had misheard God. Why was I going through this trial?

When I told people that I was hoping to start proceedings on a second adoption, only my dear friend Sylvia encouraged me to pursue my dreams. Her words were like a sweet, soothing balm to my aching, crying heart. She never swayed in her encouragement to not give up.

In the spring of 1997, when Manisha was a kindergartner, I proceeded with my adoption plans, sending in my paperwork to begin the process and half of the $12,000 required to submit the application. I had my home study updated and we began the "waiting game" in anticipation of another little girl joining our family sometime in the near future.

On a trip to Atlanta, I had my fingerprints done while visiting my extended family. A month later they were returned rejected. Over the course of the next eight months, my fingerprints were redone three more times; at the Gainesville Police Department, the Alachua County Sheriff's Office, and a fourth time at the Immigration and Naturalization Center in Jacksonville. It took eight months to get them approved.

In the meantime, an opportunity landed unexpectedly in my lap as a brand-new career was emerging on the scene. Broadcast captioning up to that point had been done on a limited scale by just a handful of companies in the nation. I had taken a test with the National Captioning Institute to see if I would meet their entry level to become a real-time broadcast captioner.

Sometimes we commit to things without knowing how much work is involved. Closed captioning was one of those things. It took hours of painstaking effort over the next five months to pass their on-air test, all while working full time and single parenting.

In my commitment to complete the captioning training and get on-air by December 1997, I had not paid a lot of attention to Manisha's schoolwork. I didn't realize how far behind she was until the end of first grade.

One day, on a rare occasion, she rode the bus home. I had walked up the street to meet her as she hopped off the steps. She handed me some papers and took off skipping down the street toward our house. I glanced through the papers and among them were her test scores from the Iowa skills.

The results were in the bottom percentile. Glen Springs Elementary had enclosed an application for her to attend summer school to help her achieve grade level before she began second grade in the fall.

I was devastated. I felt like I had failed her. How could I not have been aware? In the back of my mind, I also remembered what I had told myself. If there were health problems or school problems, I wouldn't do another adoption. I had failed the first grade as a child and I couldn't let it happen to her.

Over a year had passed since I had begun the application process. Due to all the glitches, my I-600 Petition to Classify an Orphan as an Immediate Relative still had not been approved. Many problems caused my documents to be redone multiple times. By March 1st, I had not received anything even remotely resembling a referral.

I began to have doubts if this was what God wanted me to do. In my heart, I felt like God had led me to begin the process. Why would He lead me down this road and abandon me now?

I had Manisha tested by a private school psychologist to get more information on her poor school performance. I received a comprehensive psychological evaluation a few weeks later. Based on the results, I knew there was only one choice. I would join the ranks of homeschoolers.

I gathered as much information as I could from friends at my church about homeschooling. I was a newbie, clueless as to how to do it or what materials to use.

I drove to Orlando to attend the Florida Homeschooling Convention in May. When I arrived, the parking lot was so full I couldn't park on-site. As I walked through the front door, it seemed like every homeschooling parent in Florida was there. I was completely overwhelmed.

I went to the Exhibit Hall where hundreds of exhibitors had every possible book or curriculum a homeschooler would want. I came away with one overwhelming feeling. God had called me to homeschool Manisha. I didn't know how I would do it working two jobs, single parenting, and trying to prepare for a second child, but somehow I would do it.

I joined a Christian homeschool group with experienced parents and absorbed as much as I could from their mistakes, their successes, and tried to be patient.

In April of 1998, we received a referral for a four year old little girl. I briefly thought about it but my gut reaction was I wanted a younger child. I never received any pictures.

In June, we took a vacation at the beach and my mother joined us in Jacksonville. Shortly before we left, I received a referral for a baby around ten months old. I was excited about the referral, but the adoption agency called me back soon afterwards and told me the baby tested positive for hepatitis B. I didn't know a lot about hepatitis B but the idea scared me.

I spent the vacation debating whether this was the baby God wanted me to have. The thought of homeschooling Manisha and having a baby with a significant medical condition seemed a little overwhelming.

Upon returning from vacation, I reluctantly called the adoption agency back and told them that I wasn't at peace about adopting a baby with hepatitis. I didn't like the idea of full disclosure to daycare centers and the thought of being shunned by others.

We had been homeschooling for a few weeks and Manisha was making good progress. I had hired a reading tutor during the summer that came once or twice a week and worked with her. I tried to imitate the skills the tutor used so I could be a more effective teacher.

When the hot Florida days of summer came to an end, we received our next referral, Thi My-Sa, in August. I was certain this must be the child that God had for our family because she was dark-complexioned like Manisha and could easily have passed for her sister. The pictures showed her sitting in a crib in an institutionalized setting. She had a sad demeanor and my heart was touched. She was observed being beaten at a grocery store and was rescued by onlookers.

I hoped things would move quickly and we could bring her home soon. I prayed for her daily and began to prepare for her arrival, but soon affliction would pierce my heart.

Chapter Seventeen

...Who comforts us in all our tribulation[4]

II Corinthians 1:4

On one Saturday afternoon, I heard that Disney was coming to the O'Connell Center to perform *The Wizard of Oz on Ice.*

I purchased tickets for the two of us. After a few weeks of homeschooling, I thought it would be a nice reward for Manisha's hard work.

Saturday arrived for *The Wizard of Oz on Ice* and I picked out a cute matching pair of shorts and top with ruffles for Manisha.

"Can I bring my American doll, Mommy?" She asked.

Usually I didn't want to have to keep up with the things she would later discard, but this day I told her that would be fine.

She dressed her American girl doll, Josefina, in clothes similar to what she was wearing, brushed her doll's long black hair, and made her look as beautiful as she was.

I drove to the O'Connell Center about twenty minutes from our house and parked our car at the far end of the packed parking lot. Manisha brought Josefina along as we walked up to the ticket booth. She walked over and sat down on a brick wall nearby as if she were tired. I waited in a long line to hand the attendant our tickets. A few minutes later we headed through the crowded doors. I purchased a brochure, some popcorn and Cokes. We found our seats toward the back on the second level of the bleachers.

The *Wizard of Oz on Ice* opened to flashing green and red lasers sweeping the ice with floodlights shining on the ice-skaters

---

[4] King James Version

in spectacular choreography. I was totally absorbed in the show. I glanced at Manisha occasionally to see if she was enjoying it as much as I was.

It was near the end of the show and someone tapped me on my back. I glanced around and didn't see who did it. They tapped a second time and I turned around and still couldn't see who did it. The third time they tapped me, I was growing tired of the annoyance. Then I noticed a woman pointing at Manisha.

I glanced at Manisha and it took me a moment to realize something was wrong. At first, I thought she was just staring off to the corner of the gymnasium. I glanced at where she was staring but there was nothing there. When I looked more closely, I realized there was a pool of something beside her, like water, and she wasn't moving. I called to her and she didn't respond. I shook her and she didn't respond. I grabbed her, my purse, the doll, and tried to pick her up, but I couldn't carry her and everything else.

The woman behind me that had been tapping me took Manisha from me and I gathered our things and quickly headed for the exit. The sound from the show was deafening and we fell over people in the dark trying to make our way out. It was difficult to find the exit because the seats had been rearranged and people were overflowing in the aisles. Manisha was frozen as if in a stupor.

We eventually found our way out. My new friend gently laid Manisha down on the floor. She was wet from urinating on herself. The woman looked at me and said, "I'm a neurology nurse and your daughter has had a seizure."

A security guard from the O'Connell Center ran over and the nurse told him to call 911. I crouched down beside her on the floor as she lay on her back, eyes fixated in a frozen, unblinking stare. Time stood still. I could hardly think. I wished I had a husband. I had to face something traumatic and I was going to have to do it alone.

"Where are you, God?" I cried out.

A few minutes later I heard sirens screaming. Three paramedics burst through the doors, ran over and took Manisha's pulse

"She's still alive," one of them said. "She has a pulse." They began asking me a myriad of questions.

"Has she ever had a seizure? Does she have a medical condition?" Has this ever happened?"

Manisha began to come to and looked at me sleepily. Then she began vomiting.

The paramedic asked me, "Which hospital do you want us to take her to?" They turned her over so she didn't choke on her own vomit.

I had an anxiety attack.

"You have got to stay calm. Your daughter needs you to be calm. You can't lose it now," the paramedics admonished me.

I tried hard to hold back tears.

In the depths of my soul, I again cried out to God, "Where are you? Where are you when I need you most?"

The silence was deafening.

The *Wizard of Oz on Ice* had ended and the security guards cordoned the area off to the exiting crowds.

The EMTs brought a gurney over, put Manisha on it, rolled her outside, and loaded her into the waiting ambulance.

"Shands," I said. Shands Hospital was the University of Florida Teaching Hospital. We could be there in a couple of minutes.

Manisha was crying and disoriented. The paramedic put an IV in her wrist, but she resisted and lashed out in pain. I sat beside her in the ambulance to comfort her. We pulled out of the parking lot with the siren blaring.

When we arrived, they took her out of the ambulance and wheeled her in.

"We need your insurance card," the lady in the emergency room said. I gave them Manisha's card while they took her down the hall.

"Mommy," I could hear her crying. She didn't want to lose me. She lay on the gurney watching me, agitated and scared.

Manisha's clothes were soaked through. I called my good friend, Laura, told her what had happened, and asked if she could bring Manisha a change of clothes. She promised to be there shortly.

The doctors came in and out, taking vital signs and asking me various questions. They tried to reassure me. "Probably the lasers from the show caused her to have a seizure. Everybody is allowed one unexplained seizure." It was probably nothing, they said, but they wanted to do a CAT scan to make sure.

I prayed there wasn't anything on the CAT scan. I had enough medical background from working as a court reporter and my dad's glioblastoma to know that Manisha's condition was serious. If there was something on the CAT scan, I couldn't think of anything it could be but a brain tumor. As they continued to examine Manisha, I recounted her adoption from Nepal four years earlier.

I remembered Proverbs 13:12 and recited the verse to them: "Hope deferred makes the heart sick, but when dreams come true at last, there is life and joy," and reiterated "life and joy" to make sure they heard it, but they said nothing.

The orderly pushed Manisha's gurney over to the CAT scan room. I had found a pay phone and called my mother.

Her first comment was, "Do you know what day this is?"

I remembered what day it was. September 18th. Four years to the day and almost to the hour, my father had died of a brain tumor. It was about 5:00 p.m. It was too surreal.

She promised to get the first flight out of Atlanta that she could. After the CAT scan had been done I heard the nurse calling for a doctor.

"A doctor will be with you shortly," she said and walked out. I knew something was wrong and snuck over to look at the scan.

There was something big and glowing. I nearly collapsed from fear, but the nurse returned and chastised me for being there. She quickly escorted me out without answering any of my questions.

Manisha called for me, and I hurried to the CAT scan machine where she was still lying.

"I love you and everything will be okay," I told her holding back tears. I looked into her eyes wondering what was inside her head that had caused this evil and horrible thing to happen.

I prayed, "Dear, God, please don't let her die."

A few minutes later Laura arrived with her husband, Dr. Jay

Lynch, an oncologist at Shands. They each gave me a hug. Their presence meant so much because I wasn't sure I could go it alone. Jay left to discuss with the doctors what was on the scan. Laura handed me some clean, dry clothes and I discarded the ones that were soiled.

My world, as I had known it, had been turned completely on its head. One moment I had a happy, healthy seven-year-old daughter that I loved more than anything in the world. The next moment, I feared she might die.

A pediatric neurologist had been called in to meet with me and discuss Manisha's case. Jay had returned.

"I want to do some research on something and I'll be back a little later," Jay said.

One of the nurses dripped something into her IV and walked out leaving me alone with her. Suddenly she started itching violently. I ran out of the room trying to grab someone's attention.

"Please come help my daughter," I cried. "Something is wrong. Please come now."

One of the nurses ran in and stopped running the IV.

"What is in the IV?" One of the doctor's asked.

"Dilantin."

"She must be allergic to the Dilantin. We'll have to use something else."

After that, Manisha settled down and rested more comfortably. I was shaking and scared.

"Please God," I cried, "Don't let anything else happen."

A short while later Dr. Kohrman, a pediatric neurologist, walked in. He was warm and engaging and his demeanor helped to put me at ease. He told me he had looked at the scans and wasn't sure what was going on.

Dr. Kohrman performed a neurological evaluation on Manisha. About that time Dr. Lynch returned. He and Dr. Kohrman discussed Manisha's scans in doctor lingo as I sat and listened.

Along with the neurological evaluation, Dr. Kohrman took a medical history. I told him how I had adopted Manisha when she was three from Nepal. She had chronic diarrhea when she arrived and had undergone testing to determine the cause, but nothing definitive ever showed up. It had eventually gone away with good nutrition.

She also had a stool sample with parasites, but they were never able to confirm what was there because the second stool sample was negative.

I came to appreciate how important the medical history was along with a medical examination. Both Dr. Lynch and Dr. Kohrman agreed they weren't sure what it was, but considering Manisha's background coming from a third world country, there was a possibility she had something called neurocysticerosis.

Anything that wasn't cancer had to be a better diagnosis, I thought.

"What is that?" I asked.

Dr. Kohrman explained, "Neurocysticerosis is a parasitic infection of the nervous system. It is caused by the larvae of the tapeworm, Taenia solium, normally found in pork. When the larval cysts travel to the brain, either the invasion of the organism or the death of the organism can cause symptoms, oftentimes seizures."

"Of course, we must be sure of what we're dealing with," he went on. "If it's a brain tumor, she'll need surgery. We will need to admit her so we can work her up."

I had always found uncertainty difficult. To have my child have something serious and not know what it was caused me excruciating pain. Jay took me into a private room away from the bustle of the emergency area and gave me words of encouragement and prayed for Manisha. I was thankful to have a Christian doctor and friend interceding for us.

Around midnight we were admitted to a room on the ninth floor of Shands Teaching Hospital. The ninth floor had two wings. One wing was for pediatric transplant patients and the other one was for pediatric oncology. We were assigned a room on the oncology wing. It was a nice, private room with a private bathroom.

My good friend, Sylvia Murphy, arrived late that evening from being out of town and offered to stay the night with me. I was thankful not to have to spend the night alone. My mother would be arriving the next day.

Sylvia was plump and motherly with rosy cheeks, tiny feet, and graying hair. She would often share her wisdom of raising children with me and tell me all the things I never knew I needed to know. Having her own children late in life, she took motherhood seriously, and with a wry sense of humor she could make even the most stoic person laugh.

As soon as she arrived, she fluffed Manisha's pillows and blankets, fixed her own bed, and within a few minutes, had turned the cold, white hospital room into a cozy abode of warmth and laughter.

Manisha flittered about the room basking in the attention bestowed on her from the nurses. She played with the buttons by her bed for the TV and the buttons that made the bed go up and down. Eventually she settled down and we turned the lights out. The nurses finished their chores and Sylvia quickly dozed off. I was left alone afraid and fearful. I twisted and turned unable to get comfortable; I dreaded the thought of waking up to face this nightmare.

I could hear the nurses laughing and talking outside the door at the nurses' station. I wondered if I would ever laugh again. As I stared up at the ceiling lying on a makeshift bed from a chair, I heard the closest thing to God's voice I have ever heard before or since.

The voice said, "Manisha will be okay. Lori, Manisha will be okay."

It was said twice, and the second time it was preceded by my name. As much as I wanted to believe God was speaking to me, I was too afraid. Suppose it was just my own imagination or my own wishful thinking. Unfortunately I refused to believe. As a result, I suffered immensely more than God wanted me to, but God never forced Himself on me. If I chose to be miserable, He let me make that choice.

I was unable to fall asleep because of fear and God must have thought I needed something to lighten my heavy heart. Sylvia became very animated in her sleep and I was intrigued by her strange dream as I listened to her shoot up an enemy from a tree house.

"Shoot them up, shoot them up," she kept saying. She went on for quite a while.

While Sylvia was fighting an army battalion, I was fighting a demon of fear. If only I could allow God to cast out my fears with his perfect love and make them as harmless as Sylvia's crazy dream, God's spirit of adoption would take hold and give me peace.

The next morning the hospital was buzzing with activity. Having been married to a resident at Shands in Radiation Oncology, I knew how things worked.

We met the attending physician who was accompanied by residents and students and other medical staff. Because the preliminary diagnosis was a brain tumor, Manisha was started on medication to prepare for possible surgery within a few days.

Dr. Mickle, a well-regarded pediatric neurosurgeon, stopped by. I knew him professionally having taken his deposition many times as a court reporter. Manisha would be in good hands if he did have to operate.

I asked two things of God in the first days of Manisha's hospitalization which seemed virtually impossible. I asked God for Manisha not to have cancer, and I asked God that she would not require surgery.

I couldn't bear the thought of her long, black, curly hair being shaved off and replaced with ugly stitches and scars. Memories of my dad's brain tumor and surgery flooded my thoughts and consumed me with fear. A bright and intelligent man, my father died with the mind of a three-year-old.

Later that day, I decided to do some research. I called "Information" and got the phone number for the magazine *Adoptive Families*. I had remembered seeing in the magazine a blurb for the Minnesota Health Clinic for Adopted Children. The clinic advertised a specialization in needs of adopted children. I called and asked to speak to the physician who was in charge of the clinic.

"You need to contact Dr. Margaret Hostetter," the woman on the phone answered, "but she's no longer practicing here. She is now at Yale."

They gave me her number and I called the Yale International

Adoption Clinic. To my surprise, Dr. Hostetter answered the phone. I expected to reach her secretary.

I related Manisha's story. She personally knew one of the Infectious Disease doctors at Shands and told me she would email him immediately about Manisha's case. She wanted to get him involved in case it was neurocysticerosis. She also told me, "No matter what the doctors want to do, don't do surgery." If it was neurocysticerosis, there was a possibility the surgery could spread the infection.

As I hung up the phone, I was awe-struck at how God put me into contact with her so quickly. I learned later she was Professor and Chair of the Department of Pediatrics at Yale. Over the next year I came to know her as a special human being.

Throughout the hospital stay, friends stopped by and encouraged me. Manisha was excited to have so many visitors. The neurology nurse who had rescued us at the O'Connell Center paid us a visit. I found out her last name was Miracle. The folks at the O'Connell Center gave Manisha stuffed toys from *The Wizard of Oz on Ice* (I later threw them out; it was too painful to look at them). The hospital room was overflowing with flowers and gifts, some from total strangers, who became like family and made our stay in the hospital more enjoyable. My mother arrived the second day and stayed until a hurricane began churning off the Gulf.

That afternoon after talking with Dr. Hostetter, I was anxious for the attending physician to make his rounds. I wanted to relay the information she had given me, but I didn't have to do that.

In the evening a distinguished, elderly doctor walked in who I came to know as Dr. Elia Ayoub, a professor emeritus in the Department of Pediatrics, Division of Immunology, Infectious Disease, and Allergy at the University of Florida.

Without introducing himself, he asked, "How do you know Dr. Hostetter?"

He was a kind, gentle man intrigued with Manisha's case. Shands Teaching Hospital had not had a patient admitted with neurocysticercosis for years and few doctors had seen it personally. I am sure Manisha's case had many doctors scratching their heads because doctors love "zebras." I was glad they found

Manisha's case interesting, but I wished it weren't my daughter.

Over the next several days many tests were done to come up with a differential diagnosis. She underwent a spinal tap, HIV testing, a thallium scan, tuberculosis test, chest X-ray, blood work, EEG, and the most intimidating, an MRI. They began her on anticonvulsant therapy to prevent any more seizures.

One night they handed me some information to look over about seizures. "Manisha will need to take seizure medicine for at least two years."

"Two years?" I repeated. The reality was only beginning to sink in that this was not a short-term situation that would quickly go away. It was a defining moment. There would always be the before and after, and at least for the next two years, medical follow-up would be a regular part of our lives. It was to become the norm and not the exception.

One evening a good friend of mine stopped by, Jim Norman, and I related to him that I wished I could get to a computer to learn more about neurocysticercosis. I hadn't left the hospital since Manisha had been admitted.

"We could go to the University of Florida Medical Library and check out the Internet," he suggested.

My mother took over baby-sitting duties while Jim and I walked over there. His computer skills exceeded mine and he was able to get on the Internet. This was back in the days when few people even knew what it was.

I was intrigued by an article published by the American Society of Health-System Pharmacists, Volume 5, March 15, 1998. The article was entitled, "Therapy Consultation: Albendazole versus Praziquantel for Neurocysticercosis," by Sheila S. Mehta, Susan Hatfield, Lois Jessen, and David Vogel. Jim was able to print it out and we took it back to the hospital to show Manisha's doctors.

Despite all the tests that were performed, the doctors were no closer to a definitive diagnosis. The serum and CSF antibodies from the blood work and the spinal tap were negative for neurocysticerosis. The thallium scan was negative for cancer. The TB test was negative for tuberculosis. The HIV test was negative for AIDS. It became more a diagnosis through elimination than a diagnosis from a positive finding.

The Prednisone Manisha was prescribed to reduce the swelling in her brain increased her appetite and she went to great lengths to let us know we were starving her. She gained five pounds over the next few days and began to show the puffiness in her face typical for patients on Prednisone. I found the change in her appearance alarming but was reassured it was only temporary and would go away when the Prednisone was stopped.

The doctors scheduled her for an MRI with contrast, and when the day arrived, we took the elevator down nine floors and walked outside the hospital to an adjoining building where the MRI was housed. The MRI dwarfed the room it was in. Manisha was put on her back, given an I.V. in her left hand, and the attending pushed the gurney inside an enclosed tube. The machine turned on and several minutes were filled with loud, banging, repetitive noises as she remained motionless watching a television screen.

The procedure causes some people to become claustrophobic, but Manisha handled it like a trooper, better than I did. Relieved to have it over, the nurses took us back up to her hospital room. Now we had to wait for the results.

We spent nine days in the hospital after Manisha was rushed there in the ambulance that dreadful day. She got to eat all the ice cream she wanted. I pulled her around the hospital in the little red wagon reserved for the pediatric patients. We shopped in the hospital gift store for souvenirs. Nurses came by with colorful acrylic paints for her to paint her own ceiling square. The ceiling of the pediatric ward was covered with hundreds of squares that children had painted during their hospital stay. Therapists brought in dolls that needed doctoring of their boo-boos. God blessed us with lots of friends and prayer warriors.

One night Sylvia came by to drop off my mail. In the mail were more pictures of our referral from Vietnam. I opened it up with mixed feelings. *I hope I am not replacing Manisha with this baby if she dies*, I thought. It disturbed me. My feelings were as raw as a piece of uncooked meat. I knew God was in control but I had not surrendered my anxieties to the Great Physician and Healer.

Using the protocol that Jim and I found on the Internet, the doctors started Manisha on Albendazole treatment and waited along with us for the results of the MRI. Surgery for the time being was cancelled. God had answered my first prayer!

The MRI results came back as inconclusive. The doctors discharged Manisha and asked me to bring her back in a month for a CAT scan with contrast.

Happy to be discharged, the real battle had just begun. Joyce Meyer wrote a book called *Battlefield of the Mind.* The image in the title says it all as I was battling dragons and fears that stole every ounce of joy from my life. I was terrified of another seizure. Insecurity as a single mother sapped all my energy for living and made life overwhelming. The Prednisone Manisha took to reduce swelling created a feeling of isolation because it lowered her resistance to illness and we went through several bouts of unexplained fevers. Fevers increase the risk of seizures.

I was fearful for her to be around other kids that she might catch something. The Depakote they gave her for seizure control made her sleep all the time and she was difficult to arouse. The doctors switched her to Tegretol. Tegretol can cause liver damage so she had to have routine blood testing. I was afraid she would be one of the few to have a serious reaction.

By far the hardest thing to give to God was the "not knowing." Were we giving Manisha the right treatment? If she had a brain tumor, by not doing surgery or giving her chemo, was it growing and could she mentally become like my dad? One morning when we were in the hospital, the chief resident in neurology gave me his opinion of what she had. He called it stage two astrocytoma. I dismissed it thinking what does he know? Not even the attendings would say, but it still upset me.

Well-meaning friends came to me in the next few weeks and remarked, "I didn't even recognize Manisha. She looks so different." The comments hurt. One night we went to church and some of the kids were smirking and talking in whispers about her appearance. I was worried that Manisha would overhear and be too embarrassed to go back to church. I snuck up behind every one of them and whispered that it was because of the medicine she was taking and not to talk about it.

One evening I dropped Manisha off at church for the Sunday

evening service and drove to my prayer group that was meeting in someone's home. I received a call a few minutes later that Manisha laid her head on the desk and fell asleep. I was worried she had a seizure. Could the tumor (if that's what it was) be growing? Every time she had a headache it sent me into a tailspin. The doctors finally told me it was okay for Manisha to have headaches.

Every little thing made me worry. If she was hyperactive on a particular day, I wondered if there was increased pressure in her brain and if it could cause brain damage. I was afraid to let her out of my sight in case something happened. Suppose she went swimming with some friends and had a seizure? Manisha's seizures were not petit mal seizures; they were long and protracted, partial complex seizures, requiring immediate care.

The steroids made her mean and difficult to parent. I didn't want to discipline her when she was already going through so much—with all the IVs, multiple blood draws, the long hospitalization, and the change in her appearance—how could I? And what if she died? I didn't want to remember disciplining her.

One afternoon we went for a walk and Manisha rode her bike. As we headed back to the house her breathing was labored. We paused to give her a chance to catch her breath. I worried that her weight gain was putting too much stress on her heart. She developed asthma-like symptoms and I contacted a pulmonologist to have her checked. We returned to Shands for a full pulmonary workup. It eventually went away on its own.

One night we were sitting in the pew at church and I glanced down at her and noticed a bulge on her neck. I panicked and quickly took her to the restroom. I massaged her neck and found a swollen lymph node. Two things came to mind—cat scratch fever or cancer. Our cat gave her a good scratch a couple of weeks earlier. I hoped that was all it was.

We made several trips to the doctor until it was finally decided we didn't need to biopsy it. I worried over it for too long. Manisha would kink her neck in rebellion every time I wanted to check it.

One weekend I had the grand idea to spend a couple of nights at the beach on a campout. I bought all sorts of treats and goodies and stacked them up in the living room.

The next morning Manisha woke me up.

"My neck hurts," she said.

I took her temperature and she had a fever. I quickly dressed her and took her to the emergency room fearing she had meningitis. She didn't; so much for a weekend camp-out. Many fun activities were sabotaged. I gave up trying to have any.

My fear paralyzed me and depression consumed me. My emotional state made me feel like a failure as a Christian. Prayer and reading the Bible were both difficult. There was no joy in either and my guilt over it compounded my feelings of isolation and defeatism. I resigned myself to being a joyless Christian and hoped no one knew how I felt deep down inside.

There was only one verse out of the Bible that quieted my anxious spirit. I would say it over and over to myself. It was the only verse that gave me peace. "Cast all your anxiety on Him because He cares for you" (I Peter 5:7).

A month later we returned to Shands for the CAT scan with contrast. It showed a good result so the doctors felt like we were on the right track.

However, in November, Manisha woke up one morning with a sore throat and began running a fever. I took her to her pediatrician. The nurse took a swab for strep throat and left the room, leaving us for a few minutes. As we were waiting Manisha had a seizure. I ran out of the room in a panic yelling for her doctor to come quickly. He hurried in and Manisha acted fine, but I knew she had one. He didn't believe me.

He performed a couple of breath-holding tests to see if she would have another one. She didn't. He left the room again to check the results of the throat test. Manisha seized again. I ran out and yelled for him to come. He walked back in and saw it for himself.

The nurse called Shands to consult with her pediatric neurologist. Dr. Kohrman wanted Manisha admitted back into the hospital for observation. The nurse got an ambulance and we rushed her to Shands.

This time Manisha was admitted to the pediatric floor and was in a room with three other children. I spent the night down the hall attempting to sleep on some chairs in the waiting area. All night I recited every Bible verse I could remember from memory. My anxious heart deprived me of sleep. The following day it was discovered her Tegretol level was too low.

"We need to double her dosage," the doctor told me, "and we will recheck her level in a month."

Her doctor also recommended another MRI to see how things looked. After a one-night stay in the hospital, Shands discharged Manisha with a return date the following week for another MRI.

The results of the MRI were devastating.

"No change, no change," replayed in my mind all the way home from the hospital. The doctors began questioning the diagnosis.

Manisha was placed back on a second course of Prednisone to last for four months. A second course of Albendazole was started.

The scientific literature stated for the Albendazole to be most effective, it had to be taken with fatty foods. I went to the grocery store and bought several containers of whipping cream and gave it to her three times a day with hot chocolate. I cringed because I was giving her so much fat when she had already gained over ten pounds, but because the first treatment of Albendazole had been ineffective without the fatty foods, I wanted to make sure this time it worked. I was still clinging to the hope that she had neurocysticercosis and not a brain tumor.

The next MRI wasn't scheduled until March and five long months followed October. Feeling isolated from the rest of the world physically, emotionally, and mentally, we continued with homeschooling. Nothing had happened on the adoption referral I received in August for Thi My-Sa as she waited in an orphanage. I wondered with all of Manisha's medical problems if I had made a terrible mistake. Even if things had been moving along, I didn't see how I could go to Vietnam to get her.

Emotionally I struggled. Trusting God, homeschooling, ongoing medical issues, the uncertainty of the diagnosis, and fear about whether I should continue with the adoption left me feeling overwhelmed.

In the back of my mind were financial worries. The Vietnamese adoption was a stretch. With all that had happened, I wasn't able to work as much. The bills were coming in from her nine days in the hospital, and it was time consuming to make sure every bill was accurate and my insurance paid the correct amount.

One afternoon it was raining outside and I was particularly down. I got a chair and scooted under the eve of the house and sat for several minutes watching the rain fall gently on the deck and flowers in the back yard. It was a peaceful rain and the air smelled misty. It had been a long time since I had taken a few moments to relax and have a conversation with God.

I told God how depressed I was, how uncertain I was about the future, and how worried I was about Manisha. I was tired of doctor's appointments, medicines, fevers, isolation, and homeschooling a cantankerous child on steroids. I wanted Him to end my pain and make it all go away. I knew that wasn't going to happen, but it made a difference to tell God how I felt.

Little by little God didn't take away my pain, but he helped me to realize that I had to trust Him for Manisha, I had to trust Him about the second adoption, and I had to trust Him for my finances. I had to be content in my situation. I Timothy 6:6 tell us "… godliness with contentment is great gain." I had forgotten what that was like.

So much of my worry was about me. I didn't want to be alone again. After being abandoned by my husband, I didn't want God to take my child from me. Could I still love God regardless of the outcome or would I abandon Him, my first love?

After Jesus' feeding of the five thousand, many disciples turned away from Him because they could not accept the costs associated with being His follower.

> "You do not want to leave me, too, do you?" Jesus asked the twelve. Simon Peter answered him. "Lord, to whom shall we go? You have the words of eternal life. We believe and know that you are the holy one of God" (John 6:67-60).

When my husband left me in 1985, I pleaded desperately for God to save my marriage. "I can't live without him," I cried out to Him. "I will do anything You want if You will just bring him back to me."

I lost all respect for myself and the dignity that God bestowed on me because I was created in His image.

To give that much power to someone or something is to make an idol out of it. Whether I consciously realized it or not, I had to choose who or what I loved the most. To choose anything besides God is to be deceived by the "Father of Lies" who promises happiness but delivers death.

I couldn't bargain with God. I had no rights. "The wages of sin is death..." Romans 6:23 tells us. My lack of trust in God made me feel like death had already ensnared my life because hopelessness and despair became a living hell. My joy was gone. My life was like a gymnast on a balance beam precariously in limbo of falling. If God was the beam, I had to focus my eyes on Him and keep my eyes on the beam the whole time.

A great cloud of witnesses was watching. My life was a testimony, perhaps the only testimony that some would ever see. A few nights later, after a quiet time with God, I released my greatest fear to Him.

"Dear Lord," I cried, "No matter what you choose to do with Manisha, I will love You and trust You in my pain."

Nothing extraordinary on the outside changed, but in my heart God had work to do. He had to claim back territory that I had given over to the enemy.

Jesus told John in the Book of Revelations to write to the Church in Philadelphia, "I am coming soon. Hold on to what you have, so that no one will take your crown."

To illustrate this in another way, I must tell an old family story.

Chapter Eighteen

I will search for the lost

Ezekiel 34:16

Before my mother remarried, she wanted to give Gene, her new husband-to-be, a special gift as a token of her love, but Mother was never known for her creativity. Even a mockingbird would have had a hard time imitating her off-key singing. A poetic piece about her Prince Charming would have been a comedy at best. A delectably good steak she prepared one night had Gene reaching for the Band-Aids because it was so red.

"Let's put a Band-Aid on this cow and we can get him on the road again," he said. Her lack of depth perception in avoiding cars in parking lots removed all doubt of any kind of ability to draw a three-dimensional romantic picture.

My mother wasn't blessed with a lot of originality, but there was one thing she could do well. She could knit. One day Mother arrived home with her knitting needles and bundles of yarn in an assortment of colors—reds, browns, yellows and blues, with two well-used brown soles.

"What are you going to do with that?" I asked her.

"I am going to knit a special present to give to Gene on our wedding day," she said.

Night after night I watched her work tirelessly with the long blue needles moving back and forth. Slowly a beautiful geometric shape of white and yellow diamonds emerged framed by several inches of dark brown stitches that tapered to the bottom part of the top of the slipper. When the slippers were almost complete, she attached the soles with strong black stitches so the slippers would never tear or come apart. After weeks of knitting, a beautiful pair of hand-made slippers emerged. Sewn in love and given to Gene on their wedding day, the slippers never lost their specialness.

One summer day a couple of years after my mother and father had married the next door neighbor's dog was seen carrying one of the slippers off into the woods. Much effort was made to find the slipper the neighbor dog had stolen. A local Boy Scout troop scoured the woods with us looking for it. A week past and despite all of our best efforts, the slipper wasn't found. We continued to look for it the rest of the summer but it never turned up.

The hot humid nights of summer came and went. The winds of autumn blew brightly-colored orange and yellow leaves off the trees leaving them naked and exposed. Winter rolled in and the woods around our house were silent, gray, and cold. Snow blanketed the frozen landscape like white ivory pearls and the lost slipper was forgotten.

Spring arrived once again and the harsh, gray winter receded as signs of life brought renewal. The woods around our house, adorned in the spectacular beauty of layers of white-blooming dogwoods, meant hot summer days would soon follow. The whippoorwill would once again serenade us as we caught lightening bugs in peanut butter jars.

One summer evening was different from all the rest. As we relaxed on the porch in the coolness of the day, we caught a glimpse of Gypsy as she ran out of the woods. At first we didn't notice anything unusual, but as she got closer and slowed to a trot, we could see her carrying something. It was brown with diamond geometric designs. Gypsy strode up with her head held high and plopped down the long lost slipper in front of Dad as if to say, "This belongs to you. It was stolen by a thief, but I found it and am restoring it to you."

We stared in disbelief as the slipper lay at Dad's feet after being buried under dirt and snow for a year in the woods. We never knew where she found it, but that was Gypsy. She had quite a reputation for doing the impossible.

As Dad's wedding slipper was carried off by a marauding dog, so I found myself being swept away by fear and separated from God.

> ...even though I walk through the valley of the shadow of death, I will fear no evil. For you are with me, your rod and your staff, they comfort me" (Psalms 23:4).

Once I was willing to trust God in everything, I had peace. It did, still does, and always will require a daily refilling of God's Spirit through reading my Bible, prayer, and fellowship with God and other believers. Dad passed away in 1994 and Mother gave me the slippers. For the last fourteen years I have kept them in the top of my closet. Every once in a while I will bring them down to look at them. They help me remember not only about the lost slipper, but how God restored that which was lost.

Chapter Nineteen

*There are many plans in a man's heart,
but it is the Lord's purpose that prevails*

Proverbs 19:21

Winter passed into spring and I worked hard homeschooling Manisha around my captioning schedule. The Prednisone course was tapered and stopped the first week of March. On March 29 a follow-up MRI was done that showed "significantly decreased size of a previously seen enhancing scan right frontopolar region lesion as well as significantly decreased surrounding edema," according to Ronald G. Quisling, M.D., of Shands.

Easter arrived two days later after I received the results. I praised God and thanked Him for His healing. From all appearances, it was neurocysticercosis. The second course of Albendazole had worked.

I had Manisha privately tested by her first grade teacher upon completing the second grade homeschooled, and Mrs. Adams was impressed with Manisha's academic progress. She jumped by two grade levels in both math and reading and was on grade level going into the third grade. I felt like we had gotten over the hump, and I was ready for my second daughter to join our family.

In May I took Manisha camping at the Manatee Springs State Park for a one-night camp-out. It had been a long time since we had fun together. I packed our camping gear and bought food to cook tacos on our outdoor Coleman stove.

Manatee Springs is about an hour's drive from Gainesville to Chiefland. When we arrived, I wanted to set the tent up before we headed for a swim in the cold 72-degree freshwater spring. I was worried that I had forgotten how and didn't want to be thinking about it as we swam.

I laid out the four corners of the tent several times with no success. As I was getting more and more frustrated with my ineptness, a red shoulder hawk sat on a perch a few feet away and watched. Normally hawks don't want anything to do with humans, but this one took a special interest in my activity. Maybe we were close to his nest. Maybe he was comparing me to all the other intelligent campers who knew how to put up a tent, or maybe God was reminding me "…the eyes of the Lord are on the righteous" (I Peter 3:12).

I will never know, but his piercing eyes made me feel like I was being watched. I kept my cool and eventually the tent was all in one piece. As soon as it stood tall, the red shoulder hawk flew away and I never saw him again.

A few weeks into the summer, we hosted a Japanese student who came and lived with us. We drove to Crescent Beach so Rika could experience the Atlantic Ocean. We made sand castles, jumped salty waves, and bought ice cream which melted in the hot July sun. Rika introduced us to Sushi and spoiled me with her unselfish babysitting of Manisha. When it came time for her to return to Japan, we mourned as if we had always been together.

On a whim Manisha and I went to an exotic animal show and came home with a Jack Russell puppy. After nearly a year, things were returning back to what was "normal" chaotic living for us, where I was always doing at least one too many things. In the back of my mind, however, I was antsy about my little girl who sat in a Vietnamese orphanage waiting on paperwork. Over a year had passed and nothing had been done.

One afternoon I received an unexpected letter from the adoption agency. The agency was informed a couple of months earlier by Anne, the Vietnamese facilitator, that I had to start paying $250 per month in orphanage fees. The adoption agency had paid it for two months and now they were passing the cost on to me. I was livid. It seemed like Anne was asking for money to keep Thi My-Sa in the orphanage when her job was to get my referral out of the orphanage.

I wondered if Anne was doing all she could to process the

paperwork or if there was something else going on. I also knew the adoption agency was no longer working with her on adoptions and had hired a new facilitator. Because I had already paid the total fee, I couldn't switch to the new one unless I wanted to pay another six thousand dollars, which I didn't have. A year had gone by and nothing had happened on the documentation.

By this time my I-600 Petition was on the verge of expiring and my home study had expired. I went to my church and asked some of the elders to pray. I could renege on the adoption and ask for another referral, but I was worried about what would happen to Thi My-Sa. She might spend the rest of her life in an orphanage. If I renewed my I-600 Petition and paid $250 a month for her care in the orphanage, what motivation would Anne have to make sure the officials ever processed her documents?

After much prayer, I asked the adoption agency for a new referral. I began the laborious process of redoing my I-600 Petition and updating my home study. I came close to giving up, but I still felt like God had given me the dream of a second child.

One last time I resubmitted all the documents. I went directly to the Immigration and Naturalization Service in Jacksonville to have my fingerprints redone. I was able to do the process quickly and complete it by the end of the summer.

It had been over two years since I had started the Vietnamese adoption. I received a new referral shortly after the documents were resubmitted. The referral was for a three and a half year old. Her Vietnamese name was Nguyen Thi My-Duyen,[5] and she was born on July 15, 1996. I was excited to have another referral so quickly but mentally it would take a while for my emotions to follow.

A picture via the Internet shortly arrived on my computer. The Vietnamese girl was dressed up like someone had taken the time to make her appear like a "little Vietnamese doll." I accepted the referral and began to talk with Manisha about another new baby sister. After so much time had passed, I was not sure she believed me. I was also leery about getting my hopes

---

[5] See "Bits and Pieces" at end of book for additional information

up. I had to trust God that this was the child He wanted me to have. In my heart I was still thinking about the little girl I had prayed for over a year.

September 18th came and went, marking the one-year anniversary of *The Wizard of Oz on Ice* and the fifth year since my dad's departing. Plans for me to go to Vietnam progressed quickly. The Vietnamese officials in charge of adoptions set my date for the "Giving and Receiving" Ceremony, and Kim's World Travel in Denver, Colorado, purchased my plane ticket for me to travel in the middle of October.

The Murphys agreed to take care of Manisha while I was gone. I could picture them over the holidays baking cookies and enjoying other things that I neither had the time to do nor talent for. I encouraged Sylvia to do as much homeschooling as Manisha wanted to do (which probably wouldn't be much), but I figured we could catch it up when I returned. Although I hated to leave Manisha behind, I didn't feel comfortable taking her with me. I was fearful of her having a seizure either on the plane or in a third-world country where the medical care was suspect.

It seemed as if everything was falling into place until something happened.

Chapter Twenty

Blessed are those who mourn, for they will be comforted

Matthew 5:4

One evening Manisha felt insecure so I told her she could sleep in my room on a spare cot. The next morning I was awakened by a shrill, scratching noise and asked her to stop because the noise was bothering me. She continued scratching.

A little annoyed, I woke up and said it louder, and as I did so, I glanced over to make sure she heard me. To my dismay I could see she was staring off into space with one arm draped off the side of the cot, her fingernails scratching my dresser as she breathed. I screamed in horror, "No!"

I jumped out of bed and scooped her up in my arms, as she sleepily came to. Half carrying her and half helping her to walk, I managed to scoot her over far enough in the front seat of my red Firebird to shut the door, and drove as quickly as I could to the hospital ignoring red lights and speed limits.

By the time we arrived at the emergency room, she woke up but was disoriented, not knowing where she was or what had happened. We went through another several hours of waiting until they could get to us.

After checking her Tegretol level, they discovered it was a little low. Her pediatric neurologist also wanted to do another MRI just to be sure nothing else was going on.

I was reluctant to do the MRI because it meant we would have to postpone the trip to Vietnam, but I also knew I had to do the right thing for Manisha. I cringed as I remembered the deadline looming of December 31 when the Vietnamese dossier would expire. If I did not go and complete the adoption by the end of the year, I would have to start all over. The documents were not something that could be done quickly or inexpensively. It meant I would never make it to Vietnam.

The trip was put on hold and another MRI was scheduled. The "...repeat MRI showed that the lesion had virtually disappeared, the enhancement was absent, but the edema had returned to the level of November, 1998." This prompted Dr. Carney to want to do a biopsy.[6] The only part that mattered to me was that they wanted to do surgery. I called my mother in a panic and told her what the doctors had told me.

Once again I contacted Dr. Hostetter to get her opinion, considering the pending trip to Vietnam. I was worried about Manisha and hated the thought she had swelling on her brain. There was still the possibility she could have a brain tumor. I couldn't bear to leave her behind while I traveled to Vietnam knowing things weren't right, but I couldn't risk taking her with me. I wasn't sure I wanted to adopt a second daughter if Manisha were ill. It's stressful enough to adopt a child. The bottom line was: I wouldn't do the adoption unless Manisha was okay. I wasn't sure what "okay" meant.

I also didn't know what was going to happen with Y2K. Naysayers were predicting doomsday. All I knew was that I wanted to be back to the U.S. before January 1 came around in case the computers that kept the planes from falling out of the sky froze. I didn't want to be stranded in Vietnam.

I Fed Ex'd Manisha's latest MRIs to Yale along with the original ones done a year ago, and in October, I shared with Dr. Hostetter all my concerns. She was warm and receptive in trying to help in any way she could. She made herself available on weekends and at night to talk over things and review Manisha's case in as expeditious a manner as possible.

Dr. Carney, who had recently taken over as Manisha's pediatric neurologist, was helpful in providing all the medical information needed. An accurate timeline of events was required for the consults Dr. Hostetter had called in for the workup of Manisha's case.

---

[6] Letter dated 11-5-98 from Margaret K. Hostetter, M.D.

I also offered to bring Manisha to Yale. She thought it would be helpful to examine Manisha personally and we scheduled a trip to New Haven, Connecticut, on November 16, 1999. Dr. Hostetter had arranged Dr. Sze, Dr. Cappello, Dr. Otez, and Dr. Baltimore, all experts in infectious disease and neurocysticercosis in childhood, to be available as consultants from November 16 through November 21.

We booked our plane tickets and I prayed God would do the impossible. I didn't know what that was. I could see no way for everything to work out. I wanted Manisha to be well and I thought God had called me to adopt another child. It didn't seem that either one was possible, at least not before Y2K, January 1, 2000.

Many years ago when my ex-husband was doing his residency in radiation oncology, I had been a volunteer at the Ronald McDonald House. I was told there was a House near the hospital so I made reservations. I never imagined that I would need to stay in one. The Ronald McDonald House was under renovation so they put us up in a hotel. The blessings I had given years earlier to so many families I was now to receive ten-fold in return.

My mother offered to fly up also and planned to meet us at the airport. Shortly before we left, the elders and pastor of my church laid hands on Manisha for healing and I prayed for a miracle.

We left early in the morning and arrived at the New Haven Hospital in New Haven, Connecticut, around 9:00 p.m. An hour later, a whole entourage of students and medical faculty walked in, following Dr. Hostetter on her "rounds," as she came to meet and talk with us about what would happen over the next few days. There were many tests she had scheduled. The most important was another MRI with CNS imaging, including thin cuts of the area. I was thankful to have my mother with me for emotional support.

Manisha was a trooper undergoing some complicated and at times painful tests, but the big one was the MRI. I accompanied her as they wheeled her downstairs. She did not need to be medicated, which enabled the test to be done more quickly.

The MRI machine was built differently from the one at Shands. The tube was much narrower. After she had been inside the tube for a couple of minutes, she became claustrophobic and scared. Because of the thin cuts, it took longer.

I prayed as I stood outside the clanging machine, clasping her foot that protruded from the enclosure, "Dear, God, please get her through this test without moving." If time could be measured, it would have been called "The Longest Minute."

The banging mercifully stopped and the scan was done. The nurse rolled her out of the MRI and I hugged her as she cried in my arms.

"Thank you, Lord," I spoke softly in my heart, "for helping us to get through this."

All the tests were done within two days so the third day was a long day of waiting. The doctors needed time to go through the results and examine the MRI. I knew I had done all I could. I had to leave it with God...

There is an old poem written by an unknown author called "Broken Dreams." It goes like this:

As children bring
Their broken toys
With tears for us to mend,
I brought my broken dreams to God
Because He was my Friend.
But then instead
Of leaving Him
In peace to work alone,
I hung around
And tried to help
With ways
That were my own.
At last I snatched them back
And cried,
"How can You be so slow"
"My child," He said,
"What could I do?
You never did let go."

This poem hangs in my home as a reminder to me that I must give God my dreams. If I hold on to them, God can't fix them, and if anybody has a laundry list of broken dreams, I would surely fit the bill. Not because I am "bad" but because God is not done yet. The final chapter hasn't been written. For some of us, it won't be written until we get to Heaven.

Everybody has heard the cliché, "God has a wonderful plan for our lives." My life did not seem wonderful, but that was also because God wasn't done. My ex-husband told the judge in our divorce hearing, "I took away her dreams." Maybe he thought he did, but I refused to give him that much credit. God had to delay fulfillment of my dreams until I was ready to receive them, gift wrapped by suffering, that could only be opened by willing, submissive hands for His purposes.

———————

I had always wanted to be a writer. I wrote poetry all through school and wrote my first unpublished book when I was fourteen. I relished the thought of writing a term paper and never received less than an "A."

My dreams to be a writer were dashed when I was told by my parents, "You have to do something where you can make money." The old, well-played tapes still threaten to drown out God's quieter voice that speaks to my soul. I have to turn the volume down on the world to make sure I don't miss what God is speaking to my heart.

After my dreams to be a writer were crushed, I dropped out of college and enrolled in court reporting school. I was writing, just not the kind of writing I had envisioned, but God wasn't finished.

I spent a few minutes with my calculator to discover something interesting besides how much I owe in taxes. After twenty years of court reporting and ten years of captioning, I figured I have written about one million pages in the last thirty years.

> Meaningless! Meaningless!' Says the Teacher.
> 'Utterly meaningless! Everything is meaningless
> (Ecclesiastes 1:2).

Probably ninety-nine percent of all those words, flowing from ten fingers that thump effortlessly on a magic keyboard turning funny-looking symbols into words, will burn up in the final days of God's judgment. Many of them are words I don't want to remember dating back to my court reporting days filled with depositions of people I have long forgotten and never wanted to know in the first place. I also wish to forget intimidating lawyers who argued over exhibits ranging from where to store backyard dirt to a dead cricket uncovered in a can of beans.

I have always lamented that so much of what I wrote would burn up when God cleanses the earth of sin. It was and still is a rather depressing thought that most of my court reporting or captioning is so displeasing to God[7]. I long for the day when I won't have to write sensational stories designed to tickle the ears of gullible listeners and satisfy the insatiable desires of appetites gone awry, stories that we fancy only perverts enjoy.

Broadcast captioning opened my eyes to a suffering planet that groans under the weight of greed, lust, and envy, along with a host of other sins that creation as well as human kind must endure a little while longer until Jesus' triumphant return. I could no longer turn the channel to avoid unpleasantries that I didn't want to see. I suffered immensely and still do from stories of tortured animals, murdered children, and governments who care nothing for their people. I felt in my bones the horror of 9/11 as I captioned the New York news, tears falling on my overworked

---

[7] Not the occupation, but the adversarial nature of the proceedings that take place in court and the horrid stories that captioners write reporting the news. In deference to my captioning professional friends, captioning gives the hearing-impaired public an equal opportunity to be informed in real-time, which could be life-saving. I am not casting dispersions on the profession, which is how I make my living, but just the emotional toll it can take to provide those captions. As far the court system, I know those twenty years I slaved as a court reporter God will redeem – in a future book.

hands as I tried to remain composed long enough to do my job, numbed by the evilness of terrorists who could fly planes into tall buildings.

I wanted God to take my dreams and refine them and turn them into something that would not only be bound on earth but bound in heaven. Words of hope, words of redemption, words that wouldn't burn up, wouldn't be forgotten, and would eventually reach the uttermost regions of the earth, no matter how corrupt the government. I got a glimpse of what that might mean when I was in Nepal.

God gave us His word, the Bible, so we can remember. We need to remember God's little miracles that happen every day and not be ashamed to give Him the glory. It's only through His Son that we can dream, live, hope, and breathe. We all deserve death. Now that's a story I would like to see make news headlines.

———

Today I have my chance to write what God wrote on my heart nine years ago at the New Haven Hospital, Yale College of Medicine. I was called down to Dr. Hostetter's office around 4:15 p.m. in the afternoon. I left Manisha with my mother and went alone. I had no idea what to expect. When I walked into her office, she welcomed me and asked me to sit down. She cut to the chase without any delay.

"The edema is gone!" She said. "There is only one small lesion with no edema whatsoever. There is no reason why you can't either take Manisha with you to Vietnam or leave her here and go pick up your new daughter."

Dr. Hostetter detailed in a letter written on January 3, 2000, her expert medical opinion, in consultation with experts not only at Yale but from around the country, including Patricia Wilkins at the Centers for Disease Control, and Dr. Clinton White, Chief of Infectious Disease at Baylor College of Medicine: Manisha's medical history was consistent with neurocysticercosis and not anything else; among the differential diagnoses being TB and tumor.

Something happened in my heart. I was changed and became

a believer in miracles. God used Manisha's condition to bring glory to Himself. So many people had prayed for her, I wanted to tell everyone what God had done. I did not want to be like the nine lepers where of the ten that Jesus healed, only one returned to thank Him. Not only did he thank Jesus, he praised Him loudly and threw himself at Jesus' feet. (Luke 17:11-19). Jesus said in response, "Your faith has made you well."

I could never have gone to Vietnam if Manisha had swelling or edema on her brain. As long as she stayed on anti-convulsants, Dr. Hostetter said she would be fine.

> Not only so, but we also rejoice in our sufferings, because we know that suffering produces perseverance; perseverance, character; and character, hope. And hope does not disappoint us, because God has poured out His love into our hearts by the Holy Spirit, whom He has given us (Romans 5:3-5).

I had given Manisha the middle name Hope when I adopted her. I believe God speaks to us when we name our children. As I told the doctors that night in the Shands emergency room, she was named after Proverbs 13:12, "Hope deferred makes the heart sick, but when dreams come true at least, there is life and joy." Joy was soon to follow, but not in the way I expected.

Chapter Twenty-One

Whatever you do, work at it with all your heart...

Colossians 3:23

I have always been fascinated with trains. My adoptive father, Gene, was a train collector. He liked what I call the "oversized" ones that were antiques. Although many in his collection had chipped paint and dents or otherwise looked "used," their battle scars didn't take away from their sense of intrinsic value. They represented something from the past worth remembering. Shortly after Mother and Gene married, my new dad wanted to have a special father-daughter day for just the two of us. A one-day "Fall Leaf Special" train trip from Atlanta to the North Georgia mountains had been advertised in the newspapers.

Dad purchased the tickets and I counted off the days. I told all my friends in school that I couldn't wait.

At last the day arrived and Mother woke me up early that morning to see us off. She packed us a brown paper sack lunch and bid us a good time. We drove in Dad's 1964 white Chevy to the train station in downtown Atlanta on an early Saturday morning in September. Just as we arrived, the sun poked out from behind the clouds, promising to be a beautiful sunny day.

We gave the train conductor our tickets and climbed aboard. Dad let me sit in the window seat, and I peered out waiting impatiently as other people made their way to their seats.

Eventually everyone was seated on the train and we waited. We waited some more. Nothing happened.

Suddenly we heard the crackling of the intercom and a loud voice speaking, "We are having some problems with a coupler, but we hope to have it fixed soon."

More time passed. I sat in the train staring out the window, imagining what it would be like to leave the station behind. In my mind I could hear the revving of the loud engines, the whistle blowing, and feel the lurch of the train as it moved forward, while things outside would start to peel away.

But the minutes stretched into an hour or more and the train remained still and quiet. My hopes began to fade as the long anticipated train trip seemed to slip away. The crackling of the intercom broke the silence once more as we all listened for the final verdict on the broken coupler.

"We're sorry to report that we can't fix the problem and the trip has been canceled. We deeply regret any inconvenience this has caused and hope to have it fixed soon. Please come again."

That day I learned life isn't fair. We drove home disappointed and disillusioned. In the years that followed, I thought many times about my dad and I making the trip once more, but as often happens in life, the important things get pushed aside by the "tyranny of the urgent."

In more melancholy moments, I lamented about the train trip we started but never finished. It bothered me because it was a special day set aside with Dad that never happened.

I was eight years old at the time. When I was thirty-seven, Dad was diagnosed with a brain tumor. It was a difficult time for all of us. My red Firebird must have left grooves in the pavement of I-75 from Gainesville to Atlanta as I made many trips to be with him.

One afternoon while I was in Atlanta, Mother noticed in the newspaper an advertisement for the one-day "Fall Leaf Special" train trip from Atlanta to North Georgia to enjoy the beautiful fall colors in the mountains.

"I want to make that trip," I told her. "Let's do it this fall while he is still with us."

I reminded her about the train trip we tried to take thirty years earlier that was canceled because of the broken coupler. After much prodding, she agreed. We purchased train tickets and a few weeks later I drove up once again to Atlanta from Gainesville. This time Mother would come along, also.

Snacks were prepared in brown paper bags and we made

sure Dad had his medicines, along with his cowboy hat to protect his head from the sun as a result of radiation treatments.

We arrived at the train station and I parked the van. It was a beautiful day. The darkness had given way to sunshine and I looked forward to the long anticipated event, albeit thirty years later. We made sure Dad was comfortable, had his hat on, and proceeded over to the station platform. Dad laughed and gave me a wink and a smile. I felt like time had rewound, except he had become the child and I had become the parent. I grabbed his hand to make sure he didn't get lost or fall. In so many ways it seemed like it was only yesterday that we had been at the station.

I handed the train conductor our tickets, we climbed the stairs, found a train car we liked, and sat down. I let Dad have the window seat. We sat and waited, and I stared out the window that had become like a portal looking back thirty years, waiting for the revving of the engines.

At last, the whistle blew, the train lurched forward, and the view of the outside world began to disappear faster and faster behind us, until we had left the station far behind and the world outside the train was a blur.

Dad and I shared a quiet, unspoken moment and remembered. Even though he could hardly talk, he didn't need to speak. Today we would finish our long-awaited train trip.

As we left the noise and crowded streets of Atlanta behind, suburbia was replaced by large open fields and an occasional farmhouse. The red clay became a green countryside of rolling hills and valleys, and the chugging of the train was the only thing that could be heard. Soon the world outside became an array of blurry reds and yellows as the flaming, vibrant colors of fall blanketed the trees.

There is satisfaction in never giving up and completing something one begins. I often tell my children, "Never give up on your dreams. Even if you don't accomplish everything that God sets before you, He has a plan and a purpose. The world is filled with mediocrity. Don't be like the world. In everything, you should do it as if you are doing it unto the Lord, and then give God the glory."

Like the seasons that come and go with predictability bringing saneness to our chaotic world, God brings completeness. In Isaiah 55:11, He promises that His word "will accomplish what I desire and achieve the purpose for which I sent it."

As Manisha, Mother, and I left the New Haven Hospital to return home, God had given me the truth to finish the race. In John 8:32, Jesus said, "Then you will know the truth, and the truth will set you free;" and in Proverbs 19:21, Solomon wrote, "People can make all kinds of plans, but only the Lord's plan will happen" (New Century Version).

We returned home to Gainesville with wedding bells at 30,000 feet. Manisha married the two Coke bottles as husband and wife that our stewardess had given us to drink, which promptly gave birth to baby water bottles. No matter how difficult life gets, children have a resiliency that defies logic. She never said if they were baby girls or boys, but I bet they were little girls.

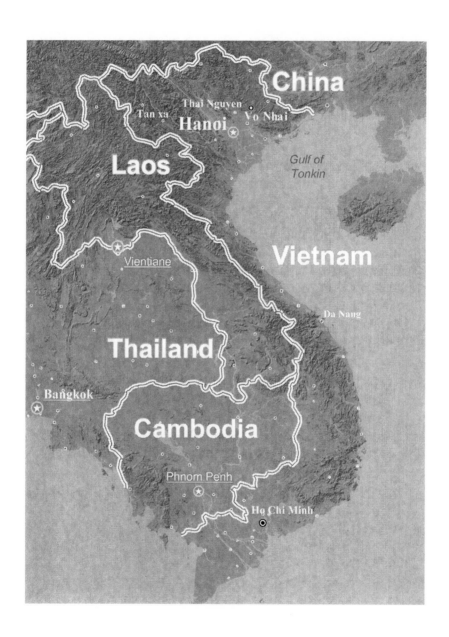

Chapter Twenty-Two

...In this world you will have trouble

John 16:33

Time passed quickly leading up to the travel date. In one week, we celebrated Thanksgiving and decorated the house for the holidays. I wrapped presents for Christmas, packed for the trip to Vietnam, gathered Manisha's clothes and toys to stay with the Murphys, paid bills, made arrangements for the care of our animals, and confirmed last-minute preparations before leaving.

I was excited to have Jenni Murphy join me on the trip. Bright and inquisitive, Jenni embraced the diversity of Vietnamese culture in a way that amazed me. Every meal was a new adventure for her in tasting the exotic. On a practical level, she became quite adept at reading Vietnamese maps—a good thing, since I was notorious for getting us lost.

I hope someday God will use the trip to reveal Himself to this talented young lady who is trained in film production. God never wastes or squanders opportunities to teach us something we wouldn't otherwise learn.

The big day finally arrived. We took two cars from Gainesville to Jacksonville. Curtis, Jenni, and Linsey rode in one car; Sylvia, Manisha and I followed them in the other. After stopping at a McDonald's for coffee, we lost each other. I figured we would eventually connect somewhere along the way, but the humor of it didn't escape me. We hadn't gone twenty miles and were already separated. How would we ever manage not to lose each other traveling halfway around the world?

After arriving at the airport, Jenni fixed the broken zipper on my suitcase that I had discovered shortly before leaving home. I could imagine all my clothes being strewn about in the baggage compartment of the plane at thirty thousand feet. We checked in my luggage and picked up our tickets, walked through the carry-on baggage check, and found the departure gate. Already fatigued with anticipation, we sat down in some empty seats and waited.

Jenni, dressed casually in her red Adidas T-shirt and jeans, had her dark brown hair cut short for convenience. Unlike me with volumes of suitcases, she had only one backpack that she carried around easily on her back. Talk about traveling light, she could be in the *Guinness Book of World Records*.

It was hard to believe the long-awaited moment was here. I tearfully hugged Manisha and said good-bye multiple times. I wished she could go with me. She told me later she cried all night the first night, but if she wanted a sister, there was no other way. I knew it would be hard, but it was harder than I imagined.

The plane began boarding and we grabbed our carry-on and stood in the long line. Jenni gave her mother and father a last hug. At eighteen, she acted grown up about it, but good-byes are always hard. I gave Manisha one more embrace with tears in my eyes, offering a silent prayer that God would bring us home safely. I blew her several kisses as I stepped up to hand the attendant my ticket, waving quickly as I distractedly followed the boarding procedures. He tore the ticket in half and handed me my seat stub.

It happened all too quickly. As Jenni and I entered the door to the gangplank, we both waved until Manisha, Sylvia, Curtis, and Linsey were lost from sight. I wanted to run back over and give Manisha one last hug. I couldn't. If Jenni hadn't been with me, I might have dashed back into the airport lobby throwing boarding protocol to the four winds. I might have changed my mind. I will never know. As I boarded the plane, my only reassurance was I knew God had called me to go to Vietnam and He would comfort Manisha while I was gone.

I also knew Curtis and Sylvia loved Manisha almost as much as I did. I laughed and thought to myself, *she may have so much fun she won't want to come back home.* She was getting a break from school and chores and I told Curtis and Sylvia she could watch all the television she wanted. "Uncle Curtis" was one of her favorite people. They could spend hours putting together puzzles or swimming in the local YMCA pool.

We found our seats, 21A and B, strapped ourselves in, and readied for takeoff. Our first stop was Atlanta. In Atlanta I called my mother from one of the pay phones as we waited. It helped to pass the time which ticked agonizingly slow. I hated uncertainty and with everything that had happened in the preceding few weeks, it was hard not to worry about the future. After the hour and fifteen minute layover in the Hartsfield International Airport, we flew to San Francisco.

In San Francisco we had two and a half hours to get a bite to eat and feel tired. From there we boarded a Cathay Pacific jet. It was a large state-of-the-art luxury jumbo jet. In three words, it was beautiful. Each of the seats in front of us had a pull-down screen with a wide variety of entertainment choices. I was fascinated with the one that showed our location in the air—our altitude, how far we had traveled, how fast we were traveling, how cold the air temperature was, the wind speed—I was mesmerized as I watched the numbers change as the plane slowly made its way toward Hong Kong.

With air time and layovers in Atlanta and San Francisco, it was about twenty hours before we landed in Hong Kong at 6:30 in the morning on December 6. Jet lagged and fatigued, we stretched our legs. I was relieved to have landed safely on solid ground.

Security at the Hong Kong airport was tight, which reminded me of when I traveled to Israel. In New York's LaGuardia, before they would let me board the El Al plane, I had been pulled out of the line and drilled for over an hour by a senior official. He along with others wanted to know why a young, blonde female, who obviously was not Jewish, would be traveling alone to Israel when the United States was fixing to launch an attack in the Middle East.

Who had packed my bags? Had they ever been out of my sight? Where was I going? How long would I be there? I wondered why other countries had so much tighter security than the United States.

In England I had been pulled out and frisked. In Switzerland they dumped out all of my belongings going through customs and demanded an explanation as to why I was carrying around a Nikonis underwater camera when Switzerland was in the middle of a snowstorm.

As we all learned on 9/11, the United States was lured into a false sense of security. This day, though, things followed a logical course and after disembarking, we found a good place to eat. The airport was spotlessly clean and beautiful. After leaving customs, the crowds thinned and we were left with a feeling of wonder at the modern, white architectural design of the building. Airy and open, adorned with much Eastern-flavored artwork in the form of sculptures and paintings, the airport was a major hub for international travelers making connections on smaller carriers.

The back side of the airport was all glass. Through the raindrops on the windows, I could barely make out the coastline of China, with the outline of huge mountains largely covered by clouds and mist. It would have been nice to see more. The little bit I could make out made me curious about what I was missing.

Before exiting the plane, the pilot had told us there were several places travelers could go in the terminal to take a hot shower and freshen up while waiting for a connecting flight. We walked around exploring in a daze and eventually found an "oasis" for relaxation. I opted for a massage in a chair that rolled bristles up and down my back and tickled my feet. I quickly settled into a couple of hours of pampering myself and enjoying a little freedom. It seemed odd not to have to worry about anybody but myself. Jenni found several shops to buy souvenirs.

"I am so excited," she said several times. "Even if we turned around and went back now, just to see this has been worth it." Her enthusiasm was contagious. She reminded me that even with weary legs, I could still feel young at heart. I had forgotten what it was like to be a college student with a zeal for the "eccentric."

After a hot shower, I sat down at a computer and typed some emails. I sent one to the Murphys letting them know we had arrived safely in Hong Kong and one to the adoption agency. "We're Almost There," I titled it. Soon it was time to leave our little pampering and board for the final leg of our journey. It was a much shorter trip to Vietnam but after flying for two days, we were both exhausted.

Upon landing and disembarking at the Hanoi airport, we stood in a long line to retrieve my bags. As we were waiting, we met two other women from Canada that were also adopting. Their adoptions required two visits and they were on their return trip to complete the Giving and Receiving Ceremony. They had already met their new daughters a few weeks earlier.

After going through customs and finding all of my bags, we dragged everything outside into the wet, humid Hanoi air to take a taxi to the Lillie Hotel. There were many vans waiting outside the airport to provide transportation for foreign tourists. We motioned for one, and a driver came over and loaded our bags into the back. I turned on the video camera as we pulled out into the overcrowded streets of Hanoi.

It had been raining and the wet streets sprayed moisture on the cab, making everything look distorted and blurry. The roads were clogged with cars, vans, motorcyclists, bicyclists, and funny-looking vehicles called xichlos. A xichlo is a three-wheeled, pedal-powered rickshaw where the driver "pumps" the rider seated in the front along the road.

Honking horns created a cacophony of noise that screamed back at me from the past. Within me an overwhelming sense of familiarity arose as I stared out the back of the taxi. *I can't believe I am doing this again,* my emotions shouted, recoiling as fear set in, and my mind, fatigued from lack of sleep, cried out, *I'm in a foreign country adopting another child!* Somehow out of this mix of chaos, fear, worry, and exhaustion a spirit of peace enveloped me. I knew God would be with me and would calm my anxious heart.

The taxi driver dropped us off on Hue Street at an inexpensive hotel. Located up two flights of brown marble-like stairs, a sign written in English advertised the "Lillie Hotel" in large tan letters. A tall Philodendron in a ceramic pot stood by the stairs. At ground level beneath the Lillie Hotel was the Ristorante Roman where we frequently ate. Jenni helped me carry my bags up the stairs, and we entered through a solid glass door that opened into a sparsely-decorated, brown-tiled foyer.

Although the hotel accommodations were rather plain, the location was attractive since Hue Street is one of the major arteries into downtown Hanoi. The hotel was also situated just a few blocks from the famed Hoan Kiem Lake, which symbolized politically and geographically the epicenter of the quaint capital of Vietnam.

Exuding warmth and charm and more conservative than South Vietnam, Hanoi had the feeling of an old-fashion town. On the north side of the lake was a labyrinth of little shops where the storeowners sold their wares. It was enjoyable to walk along the streets strolling in and out of shops. The Vietnamese women were always ready to help me find whatever I needed with a warm smile and gentleness so characteristic of their nature. They particularly catered to Western tourists and adopting families offering baby clothes and accessories at very affordable prices.

I was surprised by my first impressions of North Vietnam. I had expected to see more than just vestiges of communism as a result of the Vietnam War. Quite to the contrary, the Vietnamese had adopted a lot of our Western culture—selling our music, speaking our language, and owning their own shops, resulting in a vibrant, capitalistic economy. My uneducated mindset of a people living in apathy or without freedom was turned on its head as the North Vietnamese appeared to be hard-working and content. They showed an endearing love for their children, were kind to me, and harbored no ill-will toward Americans.

Against this backdrop of normal everyday life, having been a teenager at the height of the Vietnam War, vivid images from the past still lingered in my mind of the bloodshed spilled. It was hard to forget the nightly newsreels splattered across our television screens showing dead bodies blown apart. The horror of a country devastated by the ravages of war was seared into my consciousness. I didn't expect it to affect me so deeply after I arrived.

Everywhere were stark reminders and memorials of an era gone by. It seemed surreal to be in Hanoi. I kept waiting for a "bad guy" to show up and handcuff me. I had to remind myself that was another world, another time, and another place. A forgiving spirit over the devastation wrought on their land just a few decades earlier had brought renewal and hope. Vietnam was a land of dreams and vision for the future. Now I had come in search of mine.

Chapter Twenty-Three

This last deception will be worse than the first

Matthew 27:65
December 6, 1999, 5:00 P.M.

I felt exhilarated to have landed safely. All of our bags arrived in one piece, including the one with the broken zipper, and we checked into our room, number 504, at the Lillie Hotel without any problems. I had no tours of the red light district of downtown Hanoi as I had in Bangkok.

Aside from being tired and hungry, my adrenaline had kicked in as I anticipated receiving my baby. I walked back downstairs to the lobby to get more information from the desk clerk on when that would be. The young woman at the registration counter knew Anne, my contact person, as many adoptive mothers had previously stayed at the Lillie Hotel. I was surprised to see the other two ladies from the airport already in the lobby. They were crowded around a young man that I did not know. The young Vietnamese lad spoke very broken English

"Your baby be here soon," he said to the young lady I came to know as Jackie. She had a husband and five-year-old son back home in Canada.

So that's how it worked, I thought. Anne had a contact person at the hotel that would have the babies dropped off after the adoptive families or mothers arrived.

He looked at the second Canadian lady, who was an older woman, and said, "Your baby be here soon, too."

I was excited for them and could hardly wait to hear the same words spoken to me. My heart fluttered in anticipation to meet my new baby. This was the moment for which I had waited so long. The other mothers cleared out of my way so he could address me with news about my baby.

"There is problem with baby," he said to me.

"What?" I asked. "What problem with my baby?"

I thought he meant some sort of medical problem. My excitement to be in Vietnam and anticipation of receiving my baby evaporated into worry and fear. He started to explain more but because of his poor English I couldn't understand most of what he said. I briefly reflected back to Nepal and how fortunate I was that Ankit spoke English so well.

"When will I receive my baby?" I asked. I could feel my blood pressure rising as I tried to control the tone in my voice. The receptionist at the desk tried to help with translation, but the most I could get out of either of them was that he didn't know. Anne would call me tomorrow.

"Tomorrow?" I repeated. That was totally unacceptable.

"Please have her call me tonight," I yelled at him, "immediately!"

I was visibly upset that I was talking to him and not to her. How could she do this to me? How could she not let me know what was going on and send this guy who spoke such poor English to be the bearer of bad news? Being fatigued and jet lagged from the trip did not help. I felt slighted that the other ladies were receiving their babies and I wasn't.

The time difference made communication back to the States difficult. It was too expensive to call so we had to rely heavily on fax and email. No one had met us at the airport and I didn't know who this young man was that was speaking to me. In my anger the only word that seemed to fit was "crony."

I sent an email to Jill, the International Adoption Coordinator at the adoption agency, notifying her that we had arrived safely but there was a problem. Could she please contact Anne and have her phone me. I related to her what I knew, which wasn't much, and asked her to please find out what was going on. Nine thousand miles away, I didn't know what help she could be. The Midwest wasn't that much closer to Hanoi than Gainesville.

Because the hotel was so small, it was easy to detect other activities of the guests. I discovered the two women whom I had met earlier had their babies dropped off within the hour. I could faintly hear the sounds of a baby crying down the hallway from my room. Jenni and I sat in our hotel room not knowing what to think. I felt badly that she had accompanied me all the way to Vietnam on what was supposed to have been a wonderful experience of adoption and Vietnamese culture. We emptied our suitcases and watched Vietnamese television without interest. The excitement of being in a foreign country had lost its appeal and dissipated into emotional survival, one hour at a time.

"Maybe we will hear something good tomorrow," Jenni tried to encourage me.

"Yes, maybe," I responded, still feeling unconvinced.

Jenni quickly dozed off into sleep land but no matter how long I closed my eyes, my mind kept replaying the scenes of earlier in the day. At 3:30 a.m., wondering if anybody had sent me an email or fax, I gave up and went downstairs to the hotel lobby to check, but I found no faxes. I asked the night attendant if I could check my email using the computer in the internet room. In the middle of the night there wasn't a line waiting to access it. He turned it on and gave me the password, making a note on my account to charge the nominal fee for email use. In comparison to phone calls, it was a pithy penny, but no emails had been received in my inbox either.

I felt like we had been abandoned and forgotten. If it was 3:30 a.m. in Hanoi, it was 3:30 p.m. in Gainesville. The adoption agency would have received my fax, so why hadn't they responded? I went back up to my room and climbed into bed.

I finally succumbed to a restless sleep with lingering thoughts of the other women with their babies and fear that I may never receive mine. It seemed like only moments later that I was awakened to Jenni moving about in the room. My nightmare returned as I came back to reality.

"I am going to go down to check my email again," I told her. I grabbed some clothes, quickly dressed, and hurried back downstairs to check the computer.

I found this email sitting in my inbox from the adoption agency:

Dear Lori, I emailed Anne right after I got your fax. She has emailed me back and told me that she has been in touch with her staff person in Hanoi and the staff person staying at the hotel with you. Anne stated that their information regarding the birthmother is she is asking for money. Anne has not confirmed that so she did not want to inform you of hearsay until she has all the facts…it may be nothing, which she sincerely hopes is the case. She says it is a frequent occurrence with the distances and difficulties in communication to get misinformation and also for there to be last-minute delays. Anne assures me that they are doing everything that they can to tend to the situation. Anne said she will inform me once she has concrete information. [The director] said that oftentimes in these situations God is given the opportunity to prove Himself strong and overcome difficult situations. We are praying for God to prevail. Jill.

I had assumed I would be working with Anne when I arrived. It was upsetting to me that she wasn't in Hanoi, but as I found out later, she lived seven hundred miles south in Ho Chi Minh City. That meant I had to rely on the "crony" who spoke no English.

I shared the email with Jenni without saying anything.

"This is horrible," she replied.

"I know."

"What are you going to do?"

"Wait to hear something from Anne or Jill. What else can we do?"

Later that afternoon when we walked down to the hotel lobby, we found Anne's "crony" in a heated argument with another man. About five feet eight inches tall with medium tan skin, he wore beige slacks and a black leather bomber jacket. He couldn't have been more than twenty to twenty-five years old. The arguing was disconcerting, and I could tell he was not happy to see me. He and the other man quit arguing when they saw Jenni and me approaching.

I tried to ask him one more time for more information, but it was like asking one of my six cats to tell me which one had left an unpleasant present on my front doorstep. If anything, he only exacerbated the situation because he didn't appreciate my emotional state of mind. The young lady working at the desk tried to translate for me.

"They can't find the mother. She is hiding," is all I could understand.

"Come on," Jenni said. "Let's go get something to eat in that Italian restaurant."

We walked down the stairs to the Ristorante Roman just below the Lillie Hotel and sat down in the first booth by the window facing Hue Street. The hostess greeted us and asked us what we were doing in Vietnam, questions I didn't feel like answering. I let Jenni do the talking. We sat for a long time and I didn't say anything. Jenni let me think, and I stared out the window watching the cars and motorcycles motoring up and down the street.

The waiter brought us our food and I said a half-hearted grace, wondering where God was in all of this. Lots of things went through my mind, some of which seemed irrational. I wondered how much Jenni would understand if I tried to share some of it. I finally put my tea down, looked her dead in the eye, and said, "Jenni, I really feel like there is an Evil that is preventing me from adopting a child."

She listened intently and I wondered if she thought I was crazy. Again we didn't speak for a long time and I picked at my spaghetti and slid the meatballs around my plate. It was normally my favorite meal, but I had no appetite. Even though Jenni didn't know what to say, just her presence was comforting, knowing that she cared and was willing to listen.

Later that night back in my hotel room, the phone rang. I picked it up and it was Anne. I had hoped to hear words of encouragement but instead I was accused of causing the problem.

"If you hadn't postponed the trip, this wouldn't have happened," she berated me. "The mother was ready the last time for the adoption if you had come. Why don't you go out and have a good time sightseeing and maybe she might turn up."

I was livid! How could she suggest I go out and go sightseeing? I had waited three years and traveled nine thousand miles to adopt a child. I hung up the phone feeling outraged. "God, where are you?" I cried.

Sleep eventually overtook me but I was awakened by nightmarish, consuming anxiety. Kidnapped! In my dreams I saw myself alone in Vietnam, my arms empty. The baby that had brought me halfway around the world was gone. Visions of her being stolen flashed through my mind. I grabbed my Bible and tried to pray, but I was too consumed with anguish. I couldn't.

The next morning Jenni and I went downstairs to the restaurant inside the Lillie for a late breakfast. Between haunting dreams, jet lag, and defeatism, I was not very good company for anybody. I poured some coffee and tried to wake up.

It was all too painful to think about. Three years of waiting after filling out papers that seemed as voluminous as Florida cockroaches in the summertime, followed by refilling out the same hated documents after they expired; sharing with my friends and family my hopes and dreams; traveling halfway around the world and spending thousands of dollars; telling my daughter I was bringing her home a baby sister; all the planning, anticipation, and trusting that God would hear and answer my prayers.

I also couldn't help but think about all the people that were so negative about me adopting again. I pictured myself returning home to the humiliation and embarrassment of coming all the way here and falling prey to a kidnapping and scam—every cell in my body wanted to fight back, "No, you can't do this to me. This is evil!"

"Anne isn't doing anything to help the situation," I told Jenni. "She thinks we should go out and do some sightseeing, like that is really going to make me feel better."

"I think she is blackmailing you," said Jenni, "or it's something illegal she's not telling us, or she's already given up the baby and she's making the whole thing up. I don't like her and I don't think you should depend on her to find the mother."

"What do we do?" I asked. I didn't know whether to listen to Jenni because I wanted to believe Anne would come through for me.

"It just doesn't add up. I can tell by the translator's body language that he's withholding information and not being straight with us, not to mention he was quarreling with that other man. I assume he's another messenger. I did not like that Anne was difficult to get a hold of, and after your conversation with her, it confirms my suspicions."

"Yeah, I know," I lamented.

"Last night I couldn't sleep and really wanted something to feel connected to home," Jenni continued, setting down her drink, "and on my dresser was a paper in English that I picked up and looked at. I got to thinking and had a conversation with God. "Why not put an ad in the paper to try and find the mother ourselves?"

"Yeah, let's do it," I said. It actually sounded like a good idea and at least we would be something rather than sitting around the hotel doing nothing.

"Maybe we can ask the lady at the desk which would be the best newspaper," I suggested. We quickly finished breakfast and hurried back to the hotel lobby.

Jenni asked the receptionist, "What newspaper has the largest distribution in Hanoi?"

We explained what we wanted to do and she listened intently, showing excitement as she caught hold of our idea. She had been privy to the previous conversations with Anne's messenger and understood my desperation to do something.

The young lady showed us three or four different newspapers published in Hanoi but held up one in particular and waved it at us as she explained. She spoke only a little bit of English, but what she lacked in communication skills she made up for in kindness.

"I do what I can," she said. She handed us the newspaper and showed us where we might be able to advertise for the missing birthmother.

My lackluster opinion of Anne for the time being was put on the backburner now that I had a way to channel my frustration and anger. The bits and pieces I knew of things that happened before I arrived in Vietnam came more into focus with my raw emotions being pushed aside. I now felt angrier with myself than her because I had ignored warning signs I should have heeded, but at least now we were doing something.

By the time we came up with the wording for the notice and chose the newspaper out of the several the clerk had showed us, it was approaching the late afternoon.

"It's too late to do anything today," I told Jenni, but let's go first thing in the morning to the newspaper office."

"Sounds good," Jenni replied.

The next morning we took a taxi to the *Lao Dong Newspaper,* with the name of the "mother" of Thi My-Duyen in a carefully worded Vietnamese caption. After the cab dropped us off, we walked around for a while as we had been taken to the wrong location. Jenni had bought a translation book and was trying to speak Vietnamese to get directions from passersby. I was glad she was doing the hard work and letting me be passive.

We eventually found the right office and walked into a dimly lit room where a Vietnamese man sat at an entrance booth. We explained to him our problem and presented him with our little notice written in Vietnamese. After paying him a small amount of money, he told us it would only take a day or two to appear in the newspaper. Having finished the task, we returned to the hotel feeling satisfied.

We had now been in Hanoi for three days without hearing any encouraging news from Anne. All Jenni and I could do was wait patiently to see if our missing person's notice produced results. That evening following our trip to the *Lao Dong Newspaper,* I emailed the adoption agency and called Anne to let them know what we had done. Neither was very happy with me.

"I wish you hadn't done that," Anne said. She was very agitated and upset about it. "I told you we are doing everything we can. You need to let us handle it."

"Why not?" I asked.

She couldn't give me a good answer. Every time I asked what she was doing to find the mother, she was very evasive. The adoption agency said in an email it might cause more harm than good. I felt it was worth the risk.

As our time in Vietnam dragged on, I asked God to reveal Himself in a miraculous way. I sent out emails to friends and family asking them to join me in prayer and for God to prevail. While in Hanoi this didn't come naturally because I didn't feel like praying or spending time with God, but I did feel a sense of evil lurking behind the walls of silence that Jenni and I couldn't bridge. I also sensed the evil wanted me to feel isolated, alone, and abandoned. I felt like locking myself in my room and not showing my face to anyone. I was depressed, and humanly speaking, didn't think praying would do any good.

The one thing I had in abundance in Hanoi was time. What else could I do but pray? God was waiting on me to surrender the little girl I had come to adopt and the three long years of waiting. God knew I was a sheep in need of a Great Shepherd. I had to believe that His love for me was higher than the highest mountain, which I had seen, and deeper than the deepest ocean, which I had almost seen.

Could I believe He knew my hurt, my pain, and my anger— an adoption fiasco filled with lying, deception, and greed? I had heard about it on the Internet and television—children being stolen and sold to desperate would-be parents. I never thought it would happen to me. Jesus Himself was betrayed by one of His closest friends. Could Jesus bring redemption to this horrible injustice?

The next morning when I walked down to the lobby, I sat down and looked out the large window overlooking Hue Street. One of the adoptive mothers caught sight of me and walked over with her baby. I had intentionally avoided the other adoptive mothers because I didn't want to talk about my misfortune or tell them what had happened. It was too painful.

"Did you hear about the woman from the States who is here in Hanoi, and the 'mother' went into hiding and wants money?" She exclaimed. "Isn't that awful? It's all over the web that her baby was kidnapped! That poor lady came all the way to Vietnam for nothing—isn't it terrible? I wonder who she is."

I stared at her in disbelief. I never went to those web sites, but it angered me that so many people knew and were talking about it. How could they know more than me? After that I couldn't bear to see the other mothers with their new daughters.

As Peter denied Jesus three times and ran away in deep distress, I needed go to God and pour out my raw emotions. Did I believe that God understood my sorrow and pain? Did I believe He wouldn't leave me in this dark dungeon of doubt and depression? I was inconsolable and unfit to be around.

I left the hotel disillusioned and scurried down Hue Street to the Hoan Kiem Lake. Alone and hurting, I trudged around the lake with tears falling uncontrollably. I sobbed in anguish fearing that my dreams were gone. Passersby stared at me and a couple of women asked if they could help. I shook my head and scurried off.

As Jesus spoke to His followers in parables, I need to tell my own personal parable.

Chapter Twenty-Four

...Shall we accept good from God, and not trouble...

Job 1:10

Back many years ago, my ex-husband and I lived in Augusta, Georgia. He was in medical school at the Medical College of Augusta and I worked as a court reporter putting him through medical school. One morning on my way into work, there was a long line of cars backed up on Greene Street. Brown Court Reporting, Inc., the company I worked for, was at least several blocks down the road. People had turned off their engines and were meandering around on the road waiting.

I got out of my car and walked up the street to where some people were hanging out and asked, "What's going on?"

The man said nonchalantly, "Apparently a dog got hit by a car."

Being a dog lover, my heart welled up as I wondered how badly the dog was hurt, who he belonged to, and if he would be okay, but the man didn't know anything more.

I waited a few more minutes, not sure what to do. When it didn't look as though things would clear out any time in the immediate future, I turned around and went a different way to the office.

But throughout the morning, I kept thinking about the little dog that had been hit by a car. I wanted to know more. I walked downstairs and started checking around with some of the people in other offices on the street to find out if anybody knew what had happened. Someone told me they thought he had been transported to a local veterinarian. I scoured around and found the vet to which the poor little dog had been taken. I called to inquire.

"No," said the person on the other end. "The owner hasn't been located." They didn't know who she belonged to, but she needed immediate medical attention or she would die. Her leg had been badly injured and needed to be amputated.

"How much would that cost?" I asked.

"About $200," the woman replied.

That was a lot of money back in those days, but now that I had involved myself this much, how could I hang up the phone and not help."

"Okay," I told her. "I will pay the $200 for the surgery if she will live."

"Are you sure?" She asked me. "It's not your dog."

I was sure. My only worry was how I would explain it to my husband and what would I do with Fifi after the surgery. I knew he wouldn't want another dog.

We already had a little dog, Shelley. She was a stray who showed up on our back porch in Atlanta one day a few months after we were married. Not that much different from my childhood dog, Gypsy, who had walked into the house one evening with my dad when he returned home from buying milk. I wasn't sure if the two would get along. Shelley had never had to share us."

"When can I come by and meet her?" I asked.

"Why don't you wait till later this afternoon after the surgery?"

I spent the rest of the day imagining what the little dog looked like and how I would explain to my husband that I had rescued a dog from certain death, that the dog was an amputee, and I had paid $200 for surgery on a dog I had never even met.

Finally the veterinarian's office called and said the surgery had been successful. Fifi's leg had been amputated without complications. I could come see her but they wanted her to remain overnight for a couple of days until she was well enough for me to take her home.

"Have you heard from anybody claiming to be her owner?" I asked hopefully?

"No," she said. "We don't know who she belongs to."

Late that afternoon, I dropped by the animal hospital on the way home from work. I told them who I was, and they were glad to meet me. I gave them the check for $200 and thanked them for taking care of Fifi.

"Do you want to see her?" The tech asked me. "She is in recovery."

"Sure," I said."

They took me to an adjoining room and I poked my head in the door. Before me was a scroungy-looking tan and white terrier, with large floppy ears and strands of hair covering her closed eyelids. Fifi aptly described her, a hurt, orphaned dog in need of love and a home. She lay curled up in a little ball with one huge bandage where her back right leg used to be.

I left the vet's office with mixed emotions. I was glad I was able to save her life and give her a home, but I was wondering when I got home how I would explain it to my husband.

"You did what?" He asked me, as I was about halfway through my prepared speech, when he realized I had something more important to talk about than just the weather.

I tried to justify everything I said, saying we would find a home for Fifi and I didn't plan on keeping her. Of course, he knew me better than that, but by the time we went to bed that night, he had acquiesced and given a half-hearted yes to the new addition to the family, provided that Fifi and Shelley got along okay, which I was more than willing to accept. I would make sure of that.

Two days passed and we were able to bring Fifi home. We made her a bed and slowly introduced her to Shelley, just a few minutes at a time, several times throughout the evening. At night we crated her to keep her safe. Fifi was still wearing a wrap where her leg used to be and was still hobbling around getting used to having only three legs. After a few days we settled into a routine. I was elated that things were working out. Even my husband had quit complaining about the extra work involved.

A couple of nights later, the phone rang. It was the veterinarian's office.

"We wanted to ask you a personal question," the woman said.

"Okay," I said, not sure where this was going.

"We just wanted to know how things were working out with Fifi."

"They are working out fine," I replied. "Fifi is starting to get along well with Shelley."

"Why do you ask?" I wondered. "Did you find the owner?" Not really wanting to know.

"Oh, no," she said. "It's just that we had a client in today with his sick dog that passed away. There was nothing we could do for him. It's just a strange coincidence that Fifi looked like their dog. The old man is heartbroken," she went on, "and we thought if things hadn't worked out well, maybe you would be willing to let him have Fifi."

"We could meet and talk," I offered, "and see what happens." After I hung up the phone, I wondered if she had told him that Fifi only had three legs. Not everybody would want a three-legged animal.

The old man called me the next day and I promised to come home early from work to meet him. By this time, I wasn't sure I could let Fifi go. She had become a part of our family.

I arrived home and waited. A short while later a car pulled up in the driveway. I walked outside to greet the old man. As I watched him exit the car, I noticed something different that forced me to do a double take. He had a cane. He put the cane out to steady himself and then dragged his bad leg behind him, pulling himself out of the car with a great deal of effort. The man was a cripple.

How could I ever doubt God's providential hand? I was only the keeper of Fifi until her new master picked her up—someone that could understand what it was like to have three legs. Fifi's story would live on as a testimony to God becoming a man, fully human and fully God, but one who understands our hurts and weaknesses.

> For we do not have a High Priest who is
> unable to understand and sympathize and have a
> shared feeling with our weaknesses and infirmities
> and liability to the assaults of temptation, but One

> Who has been tempted in every respect as we are,
> yet without sinning (Hebrews 4:15).

As I paced the shoreline of the Hoan Kiem Lake, I poured my heart out to God. "You know, God, how I feel. You know." I cried for at least an hour beside the lake that had become my sanctuary. Here, among the canopy of willows, soft grass, and brightly-colored flowers, I could feel close to God and sense His presence.

Silently I told Him, "If You don't want me to have another child, I will go home and love the child that You so graciously gave to me. After three years of trying to adopt, I give up my dream. You are my God, You know best, I will not pursue this any further, and I won't be angry or bitter toward others or You."

A calming peace came over me as I sensed God's Spirit taking control of my raw emotions. He had shown me once again I must give Him my dreams. I must not let a root of bitterness take hold. I must forgive and let go. If I kept trying to force things to happen a certain way, He couldn't transform me or my dreams into something far bigger and better.

I would embrace the other adoptive parents and support them in their adoption journey. I would quit blaming Anne and the adoption agency for all the things that had gone wrong. I would be a more compassionate roommate to Jenni. I didn't understand at that moment, but God had a different plan for me. He wasn't finished, but I had to give up my dreams before He could give me His.

Chapter Twenty-Five

Every good and perfect gift is from above...

James 1:17

With a heavy heart but at peace with God, I walked back to the Lillie Hotel. As I entered the lobby, I hoped to pass through unnoticed, but the lady who had helped Jenni and me with the newspaper notice the previous day called me over.

"Look," she said. "It's in paper." She handed me the *Lao Dong Newspaper* and pointed out our ad. I couldn't read the Vietnamese part but I recognized the name.

"Wow, that was quick, wasn't it?" I said. "Thank you."

"Do you want?" She asked, and shoved the newspaper towards me.

"Sure." I took it and put it under my arm, carrying it with me to the fifth floor. Now that I had given the ad to God, I wasn't sure how I was supposed to feel. As I unlocked the door and walked in, the phone started ringing. I didn't get many phone calls, so I immediately picked it up. It was Anne on the other end.

"Lori," she said. "We don't think this adoption is going to go through. The police have found the woman and detained her for questioning. The baby isn't even her baby. The baby was kidnapped."

I wondered if the newspaper notice had anything to do with it, but I continued to listen to the voice on the other end.

"But there is a little girl who was supposed to be adopted by another family that planned to adopt two, but at the last minute, they decided to adopt only one. She was left behind. Her medical work-up has been done and except for a few minor, correctable things, she's healthy."

She filled me in on a few other details.

"The birthmother claims her baby is two and a half but she's very small and we aren't sure how accurate that is."

I failed to see how that was a negative.

"Would you be interested?"

The timing of the phone call couldn't have made it more obvious it was from God.

"Yes, of course," I replied.

Anne continued. "We have some pictures and I will email them to you. Once you receive them, call me back and tell me what you think."

I hung up the phone in disbelief. A thousand questions came to mind. Could I take her home on the original travel date? What was left to do on her paperwork? I wondered how old she really was. How could I ever doubt that God was the one in charge? He who holds the universe together could certainly hold me in the palm of His hand.

"Thank you, Jesus, thank you," I said over and over.

I couldn't wait until she sent me the email. My hope in Anne's veracity took a turn for the better, but in reality, I was now putting my faith in God rather than in man.

As Anne promised, the pictures arrived within an hour. Van Thi Trieu, who I would rename Joylin Van, was beautiful, but I couldn't see how it was possible that she could be two and a half. She was just too small. I felt like a new mother examining her "bundle of joy," counting ten fingers, ten toes, and every little feature, looking for anything that would cause concern. She had a tiny swath of hair, a cute pug nose, a movie-star's lips, and piercing Vietnamese brown eyes. A long-sleeve, striped green shirt, diaper, and no shoes were all she wore. I tried to imagine a beautiful smile across her forlorn, sad face as she was held in her birthmother's arms. I emailed Anne back that I wanted to meet her as soon as possible.

After three days of sitting at the Lillie Hotel, any more waiting seemed unbearable. For the first time since arriving, it looked like I would get to meet my new daughter. I hurried back down to the computer room on the first floor to quickly send out emails to friends and family, asking for prayer, that God would show me if this was the child He meant for me to adopt.

It was planned that my new daughter and Luu Thi Trieu, her birthmother, would come by bus to the Lillie Hotel the following day. Jenni had decided it would be helpful to get her own room to allow us more privacy. It was now a matter of waiting till "Joy" arrived. I passed the time by making the room more baby friendly, moving breakables up high, and putting anything away that little fingers might want to grab. I went shopping and purchased a few toys to add to the collection of blocks and books I had brought from home.

That evening, Jenni and I returned to the Ristorante Roman where we had eaten with such heavy hearts three nights earlier. "Maybe our newspaper ad really did the trick," Jenni commented, as I scooped up spaghetti and meatballs and she dove into some kind of unidentifiable Vietnamese cuisine.

Today as I pen these words, I wonder if that's truer than I could have imagined (see *Bits and Pieces* at the end of the book for elaboration). Spiritually, though, I credited God with defeating the powers of darkness and giving me peace even before I knew about Joy. As Psalms 118:9 says, "It is better to take refuge in the Lord than to trust in princes."

Thursday, December 9, arrived at last. Although the birthmother's village, Than xa, Vo Nhai, was only a couple of hours north of Hanoi, located in the Thai Nguyen Province, to make the bus connections and get to Hanoi was a full day's travel.

It was late evening and dark outside as I stood in the hotel lobby peering out the window. The lights from car headlights flickered off the streets and cast nighttime shadows. I had left my hotel room and come down to the lobby early because I was so anxious and fretful. It was hard to believe I had waited almost three long years for this historic moment. Joy and her birthmother would arrive soon and I nervously paced the lobby. Jenni had offered to videotape it, and when she mercifully appeared, my rattled nerves calmed down. I had been through this once before with Manisha but it didn't make it any easier. I reflected on how hard it was for Manisha when she left her father and stayed with me the first night at the Bleu Hotel.

At last three figures could be seen in the shadows walking up the stairs. Luu, holding Joy, entered through the glass doors along with Anne's two messengers whom we had previously witnessed arguing. Luu was dressed plainly and looked uncomfortable standing in the lobby. She also appeared unfamiliar with Vietnamese customs involving adoption and was reluctant to trust the man who spoke Vietnamese. Her sole source of assurance was the translator who spoke her language.

They lived in a remote area in the northern hills of Vietnam where Luu worked long hours for a pittance in a flooded rice field. Their extended family was part of the Hmong Daw ethnic group whose main population center is in China (Since returning from Vietnam I have learned that the Hmong Daw language has a written New Testament and the Old Testament is in the process of being translated. Only a very small portion of the Hmond Daw population around the world is Christian and it is considered an unreached people group according to the Joshua Project 2000).

One of the two men would translate for Luu from Hmong Daw into Vietnamese and the second messenger would translate from Vietnamese into English. I didn't know communication with the birthmother would require the translation of three languages.

It was a pregnant moment as we all stood in the lobby. None of us spoke all three languages so it was awkward to greet each other, but Joy spoke a baby language we all understood. Hers was a cry of pain. She was beautiful but her eyes were full of uncertainty and fear. She had two burn marks on the left side of her face that weren't apparent in the photographs. I was afraid to ask what the burn marks were from.

Joy was dressed in a checkered black and yellow sweater with turquoise and yellow stripes that ran horizontally. She had on bright, orange knitted pants that were too big and a yellow knit hat that covered her ears, with a little well-worn bobbin on the top.

Luu's long, dark-brown hair was pulled back in a hair tie, partially lying on her shoulder. She stood only about five feet tall as she held her baby, attempting a forced smile as she glanced at me with uncertainty. My heart went out to her, a poor, young, unwed mother, unable to provide for her baby. Would I be willing to trust her if our roles were reversed? Would I love enough to make that kind of sacrifice? I admired her bravery.

My eyes became glued on Joy. Even in the ragged clothes she wore, she was beautiful. She held on to Luu for protection as I reached out and stroked her leg over her pants. When she began crying I backed away. The two men came up and touched her and she cried louder. Luu stroked her head and gently moved her hand over the front of Joy's face in an attempt to reassure her. The more we tried to interact with her, the more she resisted.

Luu handed her a small round item and she clung to it like it would protect her, much like a child would caress a beloved toy or blanket. Tightly grabbing the object, she studied each of us, very aware that four sets of eyes were staring back at her.

Somehow I sensed that Joy knew this whole thing was about her. It was even more painful because we didn't know how to earn her trust. We found ourselves at a standoff. Jenni turned off the video recorder and we tried to think of a better way to separate Joy from her birthmother without causing her so much trauma.

Joy's wails revealed only a few lower teeth. She appeared more like a one-year-old or maybe fourteen months. I asked the translator to ask Luu her baby's age. At first she said two and a half, but she changed it to two when questioned again. It was obvious she didn't know exactly. In her village they most likely didn't keep written records of births.

After several minutes, as Joy continued crying, it became uncomfortable in the hotel lobby. Hotel guests were checking in and out and it seemed like this should be a more private affair. We decided to go up to my hotel room and give Joy and her birthmother a little more time.

It was previously arranged that Luu would leave Joy with me that night but she didn't realize that. She thought she would have her until the ceremony. The date for the Giving and Receiving wasn't set, but it was certain to be more than a week away. We needed more time to discuss things and upstairs we could relax and not feel pressured to make a quick transfer.

Joy continued to be fretful as Luu made several attempts to

breast feed her. With the two men translating back and forth between the three languages, we tried to come to a consensus. It didn't look like I would get Joy that night, but I wasn't willing to wait until the ceremony. After much discussion, Luu agreed to let me have Joy the next day in a quick exchange. She would simply hand Joy to me and leave. We felt like Luu's presence and hold on her was making it harder for everybody.

I had yet to hold her, but I could tell her skin was in poor condition. It was apparent she needed some ointment for open sores on her arms that she kept picking at. The first thing I wanted to do was take her to the doctor, have her dewormed, and get some ointment and Band-Aids to cover the wounds.

I was ready to be her new mother, longing to make her life better. Now if I could just wipe away those tears and make her "joyful," but to use an old cliché, that would be easier said than done.

Chapter Twenty-Six

...my cup overflows

Psalm 23:5

The next morning I got up early to pray. I had no way of knowing if Luu would change her mind or if she would bring Joy to the hotel. I pulled out my Bible and turned to several passages from Psalms. I ended with rereading Proverbs 13:12, "Hope deferred makes the heart sick, but when dreams come true at last, there is life and joy."

The room was quiet as I closed my eyes and contemplated the events over the past few days. I wanted the floodgates of Heaven to burst forth with angelic praise, vanquishing the evil one and casting him into the shadows from whence he came. Doesn't God promise He will overcome evil with good? In spite of corruption, greed, and deceit, because God is all-powerful and just, I prayed my heart would be filled with joy just as I longed to hold Joy. My prayers and philosophical musings were interrupted by the phone ringing.

"Your baby is here," the hotel receptionist reported.

When I went downstairs to receive my new daughter, Joy's birthmother had already left. Luu's tears of sorrow would bring me tears of happiness as Joy and I would begin our lifelong journey together as mother and daughter.

I thought of the parable of Matthew 13:45; a merchant had gone in search of fine pearls and when he found one of great value, he went and sold everything he had and bought it. The story seemed so fitting for Joy. Pearls are produced from the suffering of the mollusk as a means of survival to protect them from parasites or intruders. Joy was "my pearl of great price."

One of the translators from the night before handed Joy to

me. After three long years, my arms were full with the second of my "Children of Dreams." I carried Joy up to my room as her wails reverberated off the walls. I knew from experience the first day would be the hardest.

When was the last time I put a diaper on a baby, I wondered? I thought about my brother's messy diapers over thirty years ago. I had not bargained for the diaper routine on my way to Vietnam and Manisha was past that stage when I adopted her. This was something I couldn't have imagined in my wildest dreams when I left Gainesville—a baby. I would worry later about how I would homeschool Manisha with such a little one. This day I would celebrate my new daughter's arrival. I picked out a pretty pink dress that I had bought the previous day. The difference in her appearance was stunning with clean clothes and a quick bath.

The next thing on my to-do list was to visit the doctor and have those nasty sores on her arms and legs checked out. Much like an ant bite that has become inflamed, her little fingers wouldn't leave them alone as she scratched at them relentlessly.

In June, Joy had been brought in for a medical checkup which showed she was anemic. Luu was given medicine to treat it, but on a return appointment in October, not only did she still have the anemia, but she had also developed scabies. Anne doubted that Luu had given Joy the medicine at all and suggested I have her rechecked.

I carried Joy down to the lobby in my arms and asked the desk attendant to call a taxi for us. After the previous night's difficulty with the transfer from the birthmother, the young lady was glad to see us together. We took the taxi to the OSCAT/AEA International Clinic in Hanoi, just a few blocks from the Lillie Hotel.

The clinic had performed Joy's previous examinations and provided her medical information to me in one big packet. Blood work confirmed the anemia had not gone away, and the nurse handed me iron to give her. The clinic also prescribed medicine for her skin lesions. I bought some Band-Aids to cover the infected sores, but Joy protested loudly when she couldn't "mess" with them anymore. I cringed every time she dug her fingernails into the open wounds. It was a battle to keep replacing the Band-

Aids she pulled off with new ones long enough for the sores to heal.

"Can you write me a prescription for worms" I asked the doctor. I knew the doctors in the States wouldn't give it to me and after what I went through with Manisha, I was determined to deworm her.

The doctor surprisingly agreed. "Yes, I think that's a great idea. Everybody should deworm themselves at least every six months."

I laughed to myself. I wondered what the doctors in America would say to that. Since we were already out, we explored the area for a restaurant to get some lunch. We found one on Hue Street, close enough to the hotel we would later walk to it. I asked for a seat toward the back where I could see an American television program broadcasting in English. Several tables had leather benches that Joy could climb around on and not have to be confined to a high chair.

My new daughter's favorite thing to do was eat. She would consume the crackers and play with the utensils while we waited, and surprisingly, she was willing to try just about everything I put in front of her. Rice, however, remained her favorite food. To give me a break so I could enjoy eating, the host or hostess would often offer to hold her. The restaurant workers were always warm and friendly to the adoptive mothers. I ran into several other adoptive mothers while in Hanoi and they all told me the same thing: The restaurants would take care of their baby while they ate.

After enjoying our first meal together, I took Joy shopping for shoes and a stroller. I realized early on that nineteen pounds was too heavy to carry for long periods, and a child of fourteen months was too young to walk everywhere.

By chance, I met someone who told me about a store that sold strollers. We eventually found our way there at a leisurely pace, as I carried Joy part of the time, and I let her little legs walk as best they could some of the way. I tried to explain to the Vietnamese man, who did not speak English, exactly what it was I wanted. A few minutes later, he walked out excitedly holding what he thought I wanted. Well, not exactly. It was a baby stroller for a doll.

"No, not for my baby to push a baby in, for me to push her in," I told him.

"Okay. I see," he said in broken English. "I be back." A few minutes later he returned with the real thing. I was relieved to have something to put her in as my arms were giving out on me.

For the first five days, the only time Joy wasn't crying was when she was eating or when we were shopping, but even that wasn't stress-free. Every time a Vietnamese woman would lean down to talk to Joy, she would turn away and scream. She didn't like people looking at her. The poor Vietnamese women would look at me apologetically. I eventually told curious onlookers, "Please don't look at my daughter."

"Where is your baby's cap?" The Vietnamese mothers would stop and ask me on the street.

"I don't have one for her." *What was the deal with the cap,* I thought? It wasn't cold.

"Your baby need a cap over her head to keep her from catching cold," I was told.

After several admonishments by well-meaning, but overly-concerned Vietnamese women, I thought I better buy one if for no other reason than to honor their custom. I didn't want to be accused of child abuse. I found a shop where I bought her a pretty pink and white knit cap as well as a pair of shoes since she didn't have any.

As I squatted down and put them on her feet, Joy squirmed out of the stroller to see if she liked them. The sound of poink-poink-poink as she walked was amusing, and as I would discover later, everybody knew when she was coming. She had the distinction of being the only one in the hotel with poinky shoes.

Over the next five days we shopped and ate lots of rice. We spent quality time at the Hoan Kiem Lake since it was a pleasant place with its many park benches, and as we relaxed under the cascading, graceful willow trees, I tried to take pictures of Joy not crying.

Each afternoon following our shopping, the Vietnamese kids would greet us with their pictures, books, and postcards on their way home from school to practice their English. They would dote on Joy and hold her while they tried to get me to buy something. A twelve-year-boy took a special liking to Jenni and hung around with us for the better part of a week. One afternoon I treated him to a meal in one of the more upscale restaurants to thank him for translating on several occasions.

After purchasing clothes, bibs, Sippy cups, diapers, hats, Christmas gifts, toys, or whatever struck my fancy for the day, we would grab a bite to eat. Rice was usually on the menu, topped off with ice cream as dessert. We would arrive back at our hotel room for a nap in the early afternoon.

Joy would always cry for Va, her grandmother, before falling to sleep. I hated the crying episodes and wished she would embrace my love. Particularly distressing to me was her refusal to make eye contact with adults. She would look away in a mournful, depressing stare. After a couple of days, I lamented, "God, what can I do when she refuses to even acknowledge my presence?"

My new daughter was not ready to embrace her new reality. The pain of separation from her past, as lacking as it was, seemed better. It reminded me of the Israelites in the wilderness following their dramatic escape from Egypt, who longed for leeks and onions when God wanted to give them so much more (Numbers 11:5).

I knew Joy was sad, but I wondered if there was anything medically that might be contributing. I continued to question her age. Jill from the adoption agency faxed a list of abilities that were expected of a two year old, but Joy couldn't do any of them. By the fifth day of non-stop crying, I was frustrated and an emotional wreck due to a lack of sleep. I took her back to the OSCAT/AEA clinic and asked them what they thought.

"Could she be autistic?" I wondered.

The doctor performed a few basic tests and although she was developmentally behind, everything seemed to be there for her to eventually catch up. One perceptive, compassionate nurse grabbed my hand reassuringly and said, "I think Joy will be completely fine. Give her some time. She is just one depressed little girl."

I went back to the motel encouraged but still feeling

discouraged. I could use a lot of words to describe Joy, but joy wasn't one of them. She was the most joyless person I had ever met. How could I get her to accept me? How could I get her over "the hump"?

We also discovered she was very adept at temper tantrums. One afternoon shortly after receiving her from her birthmother, she was distressed in the hotel lobby. After much cajoling, I realized there wasn't a lot I could do to make her feel better about me or life. She would have to decide she didn't want to be so miserable. As we stood in the lobby, she yelled louder and louder to draw attention to herself. When no one took notice she stomped her feet. It was funny to see this little girl so full of anger stomping her poinky feet in defiance of the world. A couple of the people in the lobby started laughing. Joy did not like that. She stomped her feet harder as if to say, "How dare you laugh at me."

I reflected on how we are all born with a sinful nature. My new daughter was a sinner in need of a mother's love and God's salvation. I would need God's wisdom to bring such a strong-willed child into submission and obedience unto the Lord.

After several nights of not sleeping, though, I was tired, depressed, and wanted God to do something to make things better. Something had to change. I called Jenni on the phone a couple of floors below and asked if she could come to my room to pray for God to confirm I was doing the right thing. I wanted Him to take away her pain. Joy was so miserable that I couldn't bear it any longer.

We sat on the edge of the bed and prayed for the Heavenly Father to reveal His will. Later in the morning when Joy woke up, I immediately sensed a change in her spirit. She seemed "different." We got dressed and walked downstairs to the lobby. No longer crying, she stood quietly beside me in the lobby while I tended to some business.

The hotel clerk looked at Joy and remarked, "Is that Joy? She seems so different today."

Another adoptive parent made the same comment. "It's almost like she's a different child. What happened?"

I didn't tell them we had prayed, although I did wonder why

we hadn't prayed five days earlier. Now that my new daughter was more pleasant to be around, I thought Jenni would enjoy spending time with us.

Eventually each day we developed a routine. After we got dressed, Joy would gather her shoes, cap and most importantly, my keys. Usually I had tossed them somewhere in the room and she'd find them for me. After the morning scavenger hunt, she would wait at the door as if to say, "Okay, I am ready to go. Hurry up."

I would grab my purse as she pulled the knitted cap over her ears, bend down to help with her poinky shoes, lock the door, and head down the hall to the elevator. If I was too slow with makeup or deciding what I wanted to wear, she would let me know. One day before we left our hotel room, I handed Joy bottled water, an orange, and a stuffed animal. I said to her, "Which one do you want to take with you?"

She grabbed the orange. An American child would have taken the toy, but Joy had known what it was like to go hungry. Food was more valuable to her than toys. Once I realized her insecurity about food, I always gave her an orange or something to carry with her when we would leave the hotel. When she realized food was always available, her episodes of crying almost stopped.

Compared to Nepal, Vietnam wasn't much different from America. I didn't have to discuss with chickens where the toilet was, go behind a bush to use the facility, or beg for toilet paper. I didn't have to carry with me my own bottled water, and I didn't return to the hotel every afternoon smelling like dirt. There were no motorcycle rides in dresses or propositions from men that stared at me. I didn't have to explain what "caste" Joy belonged to or worry as much about getting sick.

There were things that made it hard. It was not unusual to be accosted by beggars. The most heart-breaking were those that had missing arms or legs or both. The first one that approached me had no arms or legs and I was horrified at the grotesqueness of getting around without any limbs. Hundreds of Vietnamese have been maimed by long-forgotten land mines hidden in the killing fields, many of them children.

I always lost whatever munchies I had if one of the maimed ones crossed my path as I was headed back to the hotel. My heart melted at the kind of life they had been dealt and how fortunate I was to have two arms to carry my baby and two legs to take me wherever I needed to go. After a month of giving away chips, candy, and crackers, however, I realized if I wanted that chocolate bar when I returned, I better hide it from the maimed beggars.

In so many of the countries I had traveled, I had seen a dog that looked like Gypsy. On this day, it was no different. As we walked out of a store, a little brown and white long-haired stray was scrounging along the curb where someone had discarded a plastic bag. Looking for a meal, she appeared to have been quite successful in her endeavors, as she had a few too many pounds around the waist. I snapped a picture to add to my collection of "Gypsies from around the world."

My dog Gypsy from childhood was what God had used to teach me at an early age that there was a God who loved me. Wherever I traveled, God would always bring a dog across my path that looked like her. Why, I am not sure—perhaps to remind me of His presence no matter where I traveled, or that the neediness of God's redemptive love transcended every tribe and nation.

It was the Gypsy from Israel that haunted me the most. The frightened dog couldn't quit shaking as she followed us along the streets of Jerusalem. Gypsy from Italy had a litter of puppies she was trying to raise in the island of a gas station. The one from Nepal was emaciated and covered with fleas. My dog Gypsy from childhood will come to me occasionally in dreams, completely white, as if she is waiting for me.

A few hundred feet from the Lillie Hotel was a little store akin to a 7-Eleven. Each day before turning in for the evening, we would stop in to purchase my chocolate. On the candy rack were two kinds of bars—cheap and expensive. I always bought the cheap one and dreamed about how decadent the expensive one would taste. The cheap one tasted awful, but it satisfied my chocolate addiction by leaving a horrible aftertaste. In some tortuous way, I looked forward to my chocolate every night following dinner.

Although we were routinely awakened every morning, at least it wasn't because of people throwing up as in Kathmandu. The hotel had its own resident rooster that staked its territory at the front entrance. He was faithful not to let anyone sleep past 6:00 a.m. in the morning.

After a few days of adjustment and wanting a change in scenery, Jenni, Joy, and I took a couple of afternoons and visited some of the local tourist attractions. One temple we visited was the Temple of Literature. It was built in 1070 by King Thanh Tong and later became Hanoi's first university. We experienced a flavor of ancient Vietnamese architecture as the buildings were beautifully adorned in colorful relief depicting dragons, tigers, and ancient inscriptions. There were many pagodas connected to the temple with Buddha statues out front, and the burning incense created a mystical experience. From one of the buildings, the sounds of chanting monks could be heard. I stood outside the door curiously listening, but resisted the temptation to go inside.

Outside the temple by the lake, Western-style music played via loud speakers. Several Vietnamese women had a stand set up to sell souvenirs to tourists and I bought Joy and myself a shirt. A blend of the old and the new: It was a little oasis in the midst of honking horns and city life, a charming spot to spend a few quiet moments before heading back to the hotel.

On another day, Jenni and I were invited to eat lunch at the Sofitel Metropole with the two adoptive mothers we had originally met at the airport. It was a beautiful five-star hotel a short distance from the Lillie Hotel. Out front a platform had been erected to display Santa and his snowmen, dressed in hats and scarves. The platform was decorated by a large sign with letters written in red cursive, "Season's Greetings." Santa Claus was seated on a bike with a carriage holding all the gifts. Bikes were the most common mode of transportation in Vietnam, and without snow, a bike worked better than a sleigh.

The entrance to the hotel was adorned in rows of Poinsettias, and red and yellow flowers beneath the platform framed a beautiful Christmas display. The Christmas music and decorations helped to transport me back to the familiar. At last, halfway around the world, I found myself in the Christmas spirit.

We were escorted inside and seated in a lovely Western-style restaurant. In contrast to Nepal, it was nice to share the adoption experience with other mothers and the camaraderie helped to alleviate stress. As we sat and waited, I took off my gold and silver Guess watch and allowed Joy to play with it. When my brother and sister were young, my dad would give them his watch while we waited to be served. I thought I would continue the family tradition.

A buffet lunch was served and the chef stir-fried pasta in herbs and oil. I can still taste the perfectly seasoned, spicy pasta, my favorite meal while in Vietnam. I have since learned the Sofitel Metropole has a world-renowned reputation for Vietnamese and French cuisine, even offering high-end cooking classes.

With our taste buds whetted in anticipation, we chatted and shared our adoption stories, admiring each others' new babies. The two families were from Canada, one country I hadn't visited, and I learned a little about what life was like in the far reaches of the north. Sometimes I forget, living in the Deep South, that the world's second largest country of thirty-four million people occupies a vast area of land north of the United States.

One mother showed me pictures of her home covered in snow. My mind got stuck on how cold it would be during the winter. Being born in Tampa and having lived most of my life in Florida, my thin blood would do me in for eight months out of the year.

After lunch, we took a tour of the lobby of the Sofitel Metropole. It reminded me of the Everest Hotel in Kathmandu with its stately gold columns and chandeliers gracing a high-domed ceiling. Too expensive for my pocketbook to stay overnight, it was a nice place to indulge our appetites for lunch. I hoped Joy and I could come back later for a swim. I took a peek at the Olympic-size pool and couldn't wait to dip my toes in the cool blue water.

When we returned to our hotel after lunch, I discovered my watch was missing and assumed I left it on the restaurant table. I made a quick trip back to find it, but it was gone. It was the first and last expensive watch I ever owned. I replaced it with a cheap one in Vietnam for ten dollars that lasted until I returned home.

I thought it would be fun to take a tour of the countryside surrounding Hanoi. I preferred trees, mountains and scenic vistas to the hustle and bustle of city life even though I grew up in Atlanta. I asked the young woman who worked at the front desk if she had any recommendations for a half-day excursion.

"You might like touring Bat Trang. It's a pottery village just outside Hanoi," she suggested.

That sounded like something enjoyable. I hired a taxi to take the three of us on a tour, hoping to see a little countryside along the way.

In some ways, the Hanoi scenery reminded me of Florida—flat and wet. Rice grew well in the waterlogged soil that is a food staple throughout Southeast Asia. A hard life for the field workers, it requires long hours bent over in the flooded land to tend and harvest the crop. Luu worked in the rice paddies north of us and I reflected on the future Joy would have faced had I not adopted her.

Frequently we passed bikers wearing a hat called a Non La. I was struck at how life moved at a snail's pace in third-world countries, especially away from the city. It was almost like stepping back in time. I wondered, in my fast-paced, hurried environment back home in Gainesville, what I was missing. If only I had time to stop and "smell the flowers." I vowed to spend more time in my back yard working on my half-baked nature garden when I returned home.

Bat Trang was an interesting place to visit. Established in the mid-1400s, the pottery village had a history of selling exquisite ceramics that were exported to other Asian countries. The village sits on the Red River and produces its own unique style with crackle glaze and fine glaze finishes. The pottery from Bat Trang was also distinctive in design, decorative patterns, and colored enamels.

As I write today pondering Joy's ethnicity, I wonder how much Vietnamese creativity is hidden in her genes. Joy's artistry and proclivity for creating beauty out of the absurd is mind-boggling. I wished I could have brought some of the Bat Trang pottery back, but I was too concerned it would get broken.

Later in the week we returned to the Sofitel Metropole to swim. The pool was on the top floor of the hotel enclosed in a room similar to a fancy greenhouse with sides and a top that would open when it was warm. On this day the top was open and inviting sunshine beat down on the pool's surface. I wanted to run and jump in but Joy would not go near it, crying every time I tried. I had to be content to sit with her and admire the blue, inviting water.

I reflected back to Kathmandu with Manisha at the Everest Hotel when she had found it more fun to play with my makeup than swim. On another day perhaps I might come back without her. Jenni had offered to babysit for me if I felt I needed a "mommy" break.

With camera in hand, we walked outside to a veranda that overlooked the capital. The Sofitel Metropole was situated on a high hill like a citadel. From this scenic view, Hanoi was dotted with numerous small lakes and miniature skyscrapers. As gusts of wind whipped hair in my eyes, I tried to hold the camera still long enough to snap a few quick photos. Joy was preoccupied with the long row of flower pots in front of the railing. As she looked for the last remaining vestiges of red flowers and I admired the view, one overwhelming feeling superseded everything—how God had brought so much good out of so much adversity.

I snapped several pictures of my new daughter in a pink bathing suit that I had unearthed the day before in a local shop. In her hunt for flowers, Joy had managed to find one lone red flower still clinging to the otherwise bare branches. As I held up my camera, I captured my first picture of her with a charming smile. All the others to that point showed a sad little girl with tears, a scowl or a frown. The smile for the camera, though, would continue to be rather elusive. After a quiet, restful afternoon atop one of the highest points in Hanoi, we headed back to our more modest abode on Hue Street.

Each evening before bedtime, I would fill the bathtub with water. Sitting in the warm, bubbly suds, Joy would have spent the whole evening splashing in them had I let her. I bought a couple of plastic ducks and she excitedly squeezed the little critters filling them with soapy water. Later I would have to extract the cold, soapy water trapped in their belly so the little ducks could survive another day without mildewing. Joy would have been too disappointed to lose her new bathtub friends.

One of the most frustrating things about traveling to foreign countries is when one can't speak the language. Once when I was in Mexico, I asked for towels and the maid brought me coat hangers. I tipped her for something I didn't want because I didn't want to hurt her feelings. I am also not very patient. Add into the mix an impatient little girl who easily becomes frustrated and international adoption becomes even harder.

One difference in personality between Manisha and Joy was evident early. Manisha was happy to go with the flow and enjoyed talking to everybody. Joy wanted to swim upstream and have nothing to do with anybody, but as I watched Joy play with her ducks in the tub, I could tell she was frustrated with the language barrier that separated us. It was obvious she wanted to tell me how much fun she was having. She would sit in the bath tub and try to mimic a few sounds.

I knew enough about the Vietnamese language not to even attempt it. Considering that it is tonal makes it even more difficult for non-native speakers. The doctor at the clinic had told me that Joy understood the Vietnamese commands that he gave her, which meant at fourteen months she already understood two languages, her mother tongue as well as Vietnamese.

Depravity would describe Joy's life before I received her. As she became more comfortable and not so traumatized by her new surroundings, a beautiful flower emerged displaying a gentle delicacy wrapped in beauty. It was encouraging to see her come so far in such a short amount of time.

My new daughter spent hours stacking the blocks that I had brought in my suitcase from home. Sometimes the things children do when they are young are a foretaste of greater things to come. I saw a glimpse of what made Joy who she was, her giftedness, as she patiently and meticulously stacked the blocks into various shapes and designs. When she tired of that, she would stack the pots and pans she found under the sink. I think she enjoyed hearing the clanging of them as much as playing with them.

By far the most fascinating item in our hotel room was the mirror that vertically hung on the wall. Joy rearranged my suitcase so she could sit on it in front of the mirror and make funny faces. I don't think she had ever seen herself before.

Checking out the contents of my suitcase provided interesting and new things to look at. My new daughter pulled out each piece of clothing and examined it. The only one that grabbed her attention was my bra. She tried to put it on several different ways but it didn't fit. Perhaps two might work better. She went back into my suitcase and retrieved a second one. As the first one dangled down her back, she unsuccessfully tried to put the other one over her head. Returning to the mirror and frowning at herself disapprovingly, she ran over to me as if to say, "Here, you wear these things. How does this work?"

An afternoon nap was needed each day so I could stay sane. I would put Joy down in my bed—there weren't any cribs—and snuggle up with her reassuringly. After she fell asleep, I'd grab my book from the Left Behind Series and read until she woke up. Compared to the Tribulation, living in Hanoi for a month seemed tame. At least I wasn't fighting the Anti-Christ.

In the basement of the hotel was what I called, "the dungeon." Dark and dreary, I only went down there once a day. It was the small restaurant where Jenni and I had eaten previously on that one occasion when we talked about the ad. The cook was an overly-indulgent, thin, dark-haired, middle-aged woman who went out of her way to be helpful to the guests. She knew how to make the best rice soup in the world for adoptive babies. She showed me how so I could make some for Joy in our hotel room. I never ate any, though, because it reminded me of that soupy stuff they served in the "restaurant" in the Himalayan Mountains.

One morning when I went down for breakfast I ran into one of the other adoptive mothers, Jackie, whom we had eaten with at the expensive hotel. As I walked in and sat down, I noticed her little girl, just a few months older than Joy, was walking around with a limp. When I looked closer I realized she had a club foot.

Jackie told me how excited she was that her daughter, Jenni, had started walking. Since she came from the orphanage and was crippled, she never had a chance to try. Now she couldn't wait to take Jenni home so her foot could be repaired. I marveled at how doctors could fix a limb so badly mangled. I never heard how it turned out, but I can easily imagine her running track in the Olympics.

Shopping was more fun in Vietnam than in Nepal. I didn't have to worry about running into unsightly things like dead animals hung out as food or cows and their dung in the streets. There were many stores near the hotel, and we had an abundance of shops to choose from. Most of the items were cheaply priced, especially children's clothes.

Since Joy was much younger than the one I expected to adopt, I had brought no clothes that fit her. It was a good excuse to shop, and we bought lots of cute dresses and matching knit tops and bottoms for just a couple of dollars each.

When the weather turned cool after the first week, I bought her a red coat that kept her nice and cozy, especially Christmas Eve when we were out in the night air. Joy soon discovered most of the things I bought were for her and couldn't wait to get back to the hotel to try them on.

Since it was the Christmas season, I indulged and bought some festive ornaments to decorate our hotel room. It was more fun than I thought it would be to put up strands of ribbon and a small Christmas tree. After commenting to one of the restaurant owners how much I loved the nativity scene displayed in his window, he tried to sell it to me, but it was a little out of my price range.

I didn't watch CNN—news reminded me too much of work—but after awhile, I started watching MTV. I studied classical guitar as a teenager, never having liked rock or jazz, and I was pleasantly surprised by the variety of the songs enriched with an Asian influence.

The quaint Vietnamese stores that lined the streets of downtown Hanoi were family affairs. It was quite common to see a mother and father with two or three young children out front with welcoming smiles to come in and shop. At one store I bought a beautiful twelve by fourteen inch hand-stitched picture of a Vietnamese house surrounded by mountains. A child that reminded me of Joy sat on a donkey. It was hard to choose which one I wanted but I settled on this one, because it seemed symbolic of Joy's home in Vietnam.

I also bought Joy several souvenirs, including a child's ring, a red velvet lined trinket box, and a gold and blue laced fan. I had lamented in the years since Manisha's adoption that I had not brought home more souvenirs. For the next several years, on the anniversary of Joy's arrival, I would give her one as a present to remember her "Gotcha day."

It was fun in the evenings to go for a walk when the shops were closed. The families would cook in front of their stores, which were also their homes, on little open grills. Corn on the cob was a staple. The aroma from the freshly cooked corn and other vegetables each night whet my appetite. Sometimes they would offer us some, but I always turned it down. I didn't want to get sick.

Each day brought us closer together. Despite the difficult beginning, I knew Joy was the child God meant for me to have. On December 8, 1999, at 1:40 p.m., I received this email from Jill at the adoption agency:

> I just wanted you to know that I am at home today. We are having another snowstorm. I am rejoicing in all that the Lord has worked out. It seems that you were never intended to parent that other girl, and God knew that. He knew this little one needed you to be her mommy.
>
> God is so amazing! He knew what He was doing. We just need to have faith. I just think it would be so much easier if God just clued us in a little more. But then we wouldn't have the opportunity to polish our rough spots. I hope and pray you are enjoying your time with Joy. Please try and send me your email photo. I can't wait to see her. God is all-powerful, Jill.

Jill's prayers and emails while I was in Vietnam seemed mightier than a legion of valiant warriors fighting a battle of lies, betrayal, and deceit. Only after I arrive in heaven will I know fully the demons of evil that were raging in the unseen world about me. She had just the right word to help me refocus on God even when things seemed bleak.

Everything seemed to be falling into place until...

Chapter Twenty-Seven

What is truth?

John 18:38

As time passed and I met other adoptive mothers, I became aware of "things" that worried me. The adoption agency was thousands of miles away and seemed dependent on me for all of their information, almost as if their contact with Anne was non-existent. Anne was several hundred miles south and very difficult to get hold of except through email. Email at the hotel was down as much as it was up. I was left to ponder too many things.

Sometimes ignorance is bliss. While Joy and I were enjoying our time together, there were obstacles that I eventually became aware of that were disconcerting. Looming like a huge thundercloud were continuing questions about Anne. I didn't know if I could trust her. She told me the Vietnamese government was expediting Joy's adoption. Normally taking two months, she said they promised to do it in three weeks, but they still couldn't do the ceremony until the end of December, which wasn't soon enough for me.

And what about the U.S. side of things? Once the Giving and Receiving Ceremony was held, the U.S. officials would need to approve and sign off on the paperwork. I was told by Anne they wouldn't approve the Vietnamese adoption until the end of January. Why would the Embassy be so slow? In fact, I had been told by other adoptive mothers that their adoptions were being expedited because of Y2K. The Embassy wanted adoptive families to return home before the end of the year in case there were worldwide computer failures. They didn't want families to be stuck in Vietnam. Why was I being treated differently?

I couldn't imagine missing Christmas with Manisha. I didn't have the money to leave Vietnam and come home for one day and then return. In addition, if I left Vietnam before the Giving and Receiving Ceremony, Joy would go into foster care in the orphanage. I knew that would devastate her.

Without the finalized Vietnamese adoption papers, I couldn't give Anne Power of Attorney. I realized reluctantly I had to stay until the Giving and Receiving Ceremony, which I still hoped could be done before Christmas. Then maybe the U.S. Embassy could expedite Joy's adoption like they were expediting everyone else's. I desperately wanted to be with both my children on December 25th. As I spent hours praying for one more miracle, I received a phone call from a man I later came to know as Mr. Nathan King at the U.S. Embassy.

"Ms. Roberts," he said, "you need to come to the Embassy to discuss something very important."

"What is it?" I asked. He refused to tell me over the phone.

"Please come alone and don't tell anyone you are coming."

That was easier said than done. When I asked the hotel clerk how to get to the U.S. Embassy, she must have told Anne's representative that I was going to meet with someone. Either that or someone working for her overheard the phone conversation. Shortly afterwards I received a call from Anne in which she wanted to know who had called me from the American Embassy.

"I can't remember his name," I told her. It was the truth. "But he told me to come by myself."

"I will need to send someone with you," she insisted. I wasn't in a position to protest and it made no difference to me one way or the other. I could tell in the tone of Anne's voice, however, that she wasn't happy about this new development. Was I being paranoid, I asked myself, or was there something going on that was cause for concern?

I asked Jenni if she could baby sit Joy for me so I could go and meet with Mr. King. I wanted to leave the hotel as quickly as possible and I made an appointment and took a taxi later that afternoon. Anne had a young woman who spoke very little English to accompany me. Upon my arrival at the Embassy, I introduced myself to the receptionist. She quickly picked up the phone and buzzed someone that I was waiting.

A large, handsome, middle-aged Vietnamese man stepped out of an adjoining office. He introduced himself as the Mr. King who I had spoken to on the phone. After shaking my hand and exchanging the usual pleasantries, he glanced over at the young woman who had accompanied me and the two spoke in Vietnamese. I didn't know what he said to her, but she nodded in agreement. I was motioned by Mr. King to accompany him into his office. My traveling companion remained reluctantly seated as I followed closely behind him and shut the door.

Feeling nervous and intimidated about being there, I sat down in front of his desk with a queasy feeling in my stomach.

"How has your stay in Vietnam been?" Mr. King asked me.

"It's been okay." I looked around his office which was immaculately clean and well organized.

"Where are you staying?"

"The Lillie Hotel." I was surprised he spoke such fluent English. I later learned that he had been adopted by an American family as a child and returned to Vietnam to work for the U.S. Embassy in charge of adoptions for the entire country.

He smiled and commented, "That's where a lot of families stay." We chitchatted for a couple of minutes as I told him about what had happened upon my arrival. I got the feeling as he quietly listened he already knew more than he wanted to let on. It would have been nice if he could have validated Anne's story to me about the kidnapping, but instead, the conversation took on an even more sober tone.

Leaning over his desk and looking directly into my eyes, he stated, "You must keep this confidential, but I need to inform you that Anne is under investigation by the U.S. government. I can't tell you the details, but we have grave concerns about whether your Vietnamese adoption is legal and if we can approve it under U.S. international adoption laws. We have a higher standard than Vietnam."

I sat frozen in my chair speechless.

Mr. King continued, "We would highly recommend you not leave until the approval process has been completed. If there is corruption, the U.S. Embassy will not issue Joy a Visa."

He held up several case files involving adoptions where the U.S. Government refused to issue Visas. Adopted children were left behind, stranded in Vietnam, while their parents spent thousands of dollars in legal fees. Without an American Visa, a child can't enter the United States.

"Are any of them hers?" I asked.

He refused to tell me.

"We are not processing any of her adoptions now. They won't be done until after the investigation has been completed."

I thought about all the other adoptive families I had met who arrived after me and yet were being approved ahead of me. Jenni had been right about Anne all along. It was unlikely the adoption agency even knew about the investigation. My adoption was the last one they were doing with her, and once I returned home, their business relationship would end.

Earlier I asked Anne about why it was taking so long.

"They won't be able to finish your paperwork till the end of January," was all she would say.

"What is holding up my case? Other adoptive families who arrived after me are being processed by the U.S. Embassy almost immediately," I tried to tell her.

"That's not possible," she said.

I could take Joy home before the end of the year if they would do my paperwork like everybody else, I lamented. Anne continued to be evasive, but she did offer to escort Joy home for no charge along with some other children.

Suppose I couldn't adopt Joy after all, I thought to myself, as I sensed a veil of evilness in all of it. Satan, the father of lies, had done everything he could do to stop me from adopting in Vietnam. God, the Author and Father of Truth, would have to swallow evil up in victory. I had to believe. As the man said to Jesus in Mark 8:24 concerning his son, "I do believe; help me overcome my unbelief!"

Many times I had almost given up. Would I be afraid to love Joy, fearful that things might fall through? I thought of Romans 8:15. God, my heavenly Father, had traveled this road with me before. Was there too much of my fearful self wrapped up in this and not enough of Him?

Mr. King warned, "Stay in Vietnam until we complete our investigation, and be careful in your dealing with Anne."

Uncertainty consumed me. Mr. King gave me his name and phone number and told me to call him if I had any questions. As I walked out of the office, I looked away from the woman who had accompanied me. I didn't know what to say to her.

Jenni had offered to change her plane ticket and stay with me until I left, but I knew Sylvia and Curtis would want her to come home for Christmas. I also knew if she left she could take pictures back of Joy. Even though I missed Manisha immensely, I felt like this Christmas Joy needed me more than she did. I had to trust God because I had no control over the U.S. Embassy. As I had done with Manisha's adoption, I had to render under Caesar the things that were Caesar's and render unto God the things that were God's.

My flight was booked to leave Hanoi on December 30. I would arrive home just before 2000 when Y2K would hit and all my documents would expire. Joy's adoption had taken to the very last possible day of the millennium. If one other thing had happened to cause a delay, I wouldn't have been able to adopt her. If Manisha had not had a miraculous healing, I wouldn't have been able to come to Vietnam at all. If the U.S. Embassy found something wrong with Joy's adoption or with something Anne had done, she would never be able to leave Vietnam.

I continued to wonder about the little girl that sat in the orphanage whose paperwork was never completed. What about the little girl I came to Vietnam to adopt? Years later, I would realize the truth, not just as head knowledge, but in my heart, that "… in all things God works for the good of those who love him, who have been called according to his purpose" (Romans 8:28).

I had to put my trust in God, despite the evil which prowled around like a hungry lion. As I pondered these things in my heart, I was determined not to give in to worry. Certainly that came easier to me than prayer on the heels of Mr. King's admonition, but I would pray to keep away the demons that threatened to take away my dreams. I had to cling to the hope that in spite of everything, Joy was the daughter God meant me to have.

Her name seemed so fitting at Christmas. Galatians 6:7 says,

"Do not be deceived: God cannot be mocked." Was it not part of God's plan for me to be in Hanoi at Christmas and adopt a little girl named Joy?

I was determined to remain positive and thought about having a late Christmas with Manisha when I returned home. Christmas doesn't have to be on December 25. On December 19, I sent this email to Manisha.

> Dear Manisha, I love you and miss you, too. I wish I could be home for Christmas. I could have, but it would have been so hard to come back and expensive, and we might not have gotten Joy. I prayed and I knew God would take care of you, along with Uncle Curtis and Auntie Sylvia. Pray for God to bring Jenni and me home safe. Lots of hugs and kisses, Mom.

Chapter Twenty-Eight

Glory to God in the highest, and on earth peace to men...

Luke 2:14

By the time December 21 rolled around, I think Jenni had her fill of "tasting the culture." She had crashed in a xichlo, visited the school where her 12-year-old little translator attended, spent some time with Australian backpackers, and ate exotic fish cooked in honey at a hole in a wall.

When she left, most of the other adoptive families were also gone. The hotel was largely empty and quiet. It was too expensive to call home often, so I sent emails every day to all my prayer warriors. The highlight each day was my email from Sylvia about all the holiday activities—baking Christmas cookies, shopping at the mall, cutting down a Christmas tree, wrapping presents, and watching several movies at the theater. I knew they couldn't take my place but Manisha would have a wonderful Christmas.

Tired of being a tourist, time goes by slowly when you can't do what you want. The shops were closed for the holidays and few restaurants were open. For the first time in years I was bored; the boredom was far worse than being too busy.

God had His way in using what I considered a waste of time to bring redemption. Staying the extra nine days in Vietnam gave the two of us as mother and daughter hours together without the distractions of daily living in a hectic world back home. We spent hours each day playing with blocks and at night I would read to Joy from some books I had brought. I lavished her with lots of hugs and kisses, and as she thrived on the attention, her insecure, little personality began to peek out. She was now smiling and for the first time in her short life had all of her needs met. Even the little sores on her arms that she had picked at in the beginning were going away and three new teeth were visible.

The Giving and Receiving Ceremony was scheduled for December 24th, Christmas Eve, but was delayed to December 27th—three more days of waiting. It eliminated any chance for all of us to be together on Christmas. I was left with counting down each day knowing I was one step closer to coming home. In quiet moments I reflected on the Bing Crosby song, *I'll be home for Christmas, if only in my dreams.*

I asked several people if they knew of a Christmas Eve service we could attend, but because Vietnam is communist and Christians are persecuted, nobody was very forthcoming. One person told me about a sanctioned church service, but that it probably wouldn't be what I wanted. Anything seemed better than nothing, and without giving it much thought, I made plans to go.

It was Christmas Eve, December 24, and we dressed up for the occasion anticipating something memorable. I called a taxi and gave the name of the location to the driver. He dropped us off at a church that appeared to be at least several hundred years old.

We walked in and the sanctuary was packed with a large crowd seated in pews. A man in a robe at the front was conducting the service in another language besides Vietnamese; maybe it was Latin. His voice reverberated and echoed off the ancient walls of the building and the chanting put me ill at ease. I was disappointed for having gone to the trouble of coming and had no desire to stay. We left after several minutes and returned to the hotel.

As we entered the hotel lobby, I was greeted by the young woman who was working the night shift. Despite not being home with her family, she was cheery and festive.

"Here is a present for you," she said to me with a big smile. She pointed to it on the counter. "You are back so soon?"

"Yes, it wasn't what I thought it would be, but what is this?" I picked up the present and eyed it with a sense of wonder. I couldn't believe someone had thought of me for Christmas. It made being away from home almost bearable. The present was beautifully wrapped in green Christmas paper.

"It's Christmas, isn't it? She answered, "Your custom?"

"Yes. Can I open it now?" I asked.

"Yes, please do."

I unwrapped the small gift and hidden inside were two handmade white doilies, one for a cup and the other for a plate, lined in green stitching along the outside edges.

"Thank you; they are beautiful."

"You are welcome," she beamed back. It was a special moment in what otherwise had seemed like a gloomy day.

"Merry Christmas," I said. "I am sorry you have to work." I knew she had two kids at home, but I wasn't sure if they celebrated Christmas.

"It's okay," she said.

We said good night, and Joy and I headed back up to our room. I thought we would spend a quiet evening watching CNN and MTV, but as always, at least for me, there is the rest of the story. After feeling sorry for myself and moping around for an hour, I called the Murphys. It was late enough I hoped I wouldn't wake them up, but I couldn't wait any longer.

"Merry Christmas!" I shouted excitedly into the phone. A lot of love can be shared in a short amount of time. Manisha was happy to talk to me and told me about all the things Santa had brought her.

"When are you coming home? I miss you," she said.

"I miss you, too, Honey. I will be home soon."

I thought in my heart, though, not soon enough. Tears welled up in my eyes as I regretted that I couldn't be with both my daughters for Christmas. Jenni had shared the pictures of Joy with Manisha and I hoped she could focus on meeting her new baby sister. It was a short conversation, but I felt better having heard her sweet voice across the ocean, reminding me that although we weren't together in person, she was with me in spirit.

As I watched television feeling homesick, I heard noises outside, louder than the usual honking of horns and vehicular traffic. I picked up Joy and we walked back downstairs to the lobby. I felt excitement in the air with faint Christmas music barely audible above the sporadic street noise.

"What's going on?" I asked the young lady who had given me the gift earlier.

"It's the Christmas celebration," she said.

What celebration? I thought to myself. Vietnam is a communist country and they don't celebrate Christmas, or so I thought.

I quickly ran back up to our room, grabbed our coats and stroller, and carried Joy down the steps into the cool night air. I could see crowds up ahead on Hue Street walking toward Hoan Kiem Lake. We joined the crowd, and as we approached, Hanoi's version of Christmas spread out before us. The lake was decorated with Christmas lights, and a large Christmas tree adorned with presents took center stage. A cardboard Santa Claus was displayed near the tree. A little baby swing decorated in a colorful leis was set up to take pictures.

Crowds gathered in the streets wearing red Santa stocking caps and carrying balloons. I couldn't decide if the "party" resembled a parade or people gathering for a concert. A festive, family atmosphere filled the air, and the lake was packed with Vietnamese families.

I was excited to have something to do. Uplifting, holiday music wafted from the loud speakers over the noisy crowd. I wanted to know where the music was coming from. It had a sweet-sounding familiarity, like a piece of chocolate to a hungry soul. I wanted to grab it and not let go.

In such an anti-Christian country, I never thought I would hear Christmas music broadcast in downtown Hanoi. Many of our Christmas songs have a message of "tidings of great joy," with Jesus as a baby in the manger. Even though the celebration was steeped in commercialism, the familiar words from Christmas carols filled the air, giving me hope that all was well with my soul. I pushed Joy in her stroller to the nearby church a few hundred feet from where the music came.

My soul was enraptured with joy, a balm for my homesick heart. I longed to be with friends and family. Here I could sing in harmony, filled with the Christmas spirit, enveloped in oneness with those around me who were here for a different experience, but so far from home, I welcomed Christmas in another culture.

For a brief moment, I understood Ephesians 4:5. There is unity in the world, "one body, one hope, one baptism, one God and father of all." I felt a connection to the Vietnamese people. For some, this might be the only testimony to the risen Savior they would ever witness, but as Isaiah 56:11 says, "My word...will not return to me empty."

As the crowds swelled, Joy's stroller became a nuisance as several men tripped over it in the sea of people. I also felt someone's hand sliding down the back of my pant pocket. I knew we needed to go, but God had given me a taste of Christmas in Hanoi that I would always treasure. We returned to the Lake and I took Joy over to the Christmas tree and swing. She was intrigued with the bobbing balloons tied to the Santa and stared wide-eyed at the Christmas lights strung around. I handed the camera to someone to take our picture. Standing in front of a cardboard Santa Claus, the bittersweet moment was captured, now kept in the scrapbook that I had won years earlier, a memoir to the past I didn't want to forget.

Chapter Twenty-Nine

Choose Life, then, that you and your descendants may live

Deuteronomy 30:19

On December 26, the day after Christmas, Joy and I walked out of the Lillie Hotel to rays of sunshine glistening off the street pavement. I had finally become accustomed to checking at least four times before crossing the street since the heavy traffic would not yield to pedestrians. Frequently Joy's stroller would get stuck going up and down the uneven curb or land in a deep gutter. After Jenni's collision in a xichlo, my favorite *Star Trek* line was resurrected from childhood. We were going "where no man (or woman) had gone before" every time we crossed a road in downtown Hanoi.

The heavy cloud of disappointment that had settled over me because I couldn't take Joy home for Christmas had now lifted since the holidays were behind us. I looked ahead with hope and expectation to the Giving and Receiving Ceremony two days away. It was easier to enjoy sightseeing now that the adoption day was near and my time to return home would soon follow.

We had become mother and daughter during our two weeks together. The days lazily spent at the park and shopping had provided hours of nurturing and bonding with Joy and an opportunity for me to experience the blessedness of motherhood once again. Almond eyes, straight black hair, and a pug nose didn't represent just any little Vietnamese girl I saw on the street—they were Joy's, my daughter from Vietnam.

During our daily outings as we strolled along the streets, my conscience had been seared by the many war memorials that were part of the landscape of Hanoi, a tribute to the distant past. On the streets were reminders "to never forget." The well-preserved relics were like anachronistic objects woefully out of place and time in a world that had moved on. Forgiveness and healing had replaced the pain, but lest we forget our past and those who died, everywhere were remembrances.

We visited the Hoa Lo Prison, meaning "coal oven," and also known as the *Hanoi Hilton*. From 1964 to 1973, the Hoa Lo Prison housed American prisoners of war, among the more famous, John McCain. Pictures and writings only told part of the story. I could only imagine the atrocities and torture that were committed.

We didn't stay long as the pictures and solemnity reminded me of Yad Vashem in Jerusalem, a memorial to the six million Jews who were brutally murdered in the Holocaust. It filled me with too much sadness that I didn't want to dwell on, but I silently thanked the American soldiers who gave their lives. Coming to the Hoa Lo Prison was my way of bearing witness to the unsung heroes who sacrificed so much. We also toured the Bao Tang Quan Doi or Army Museum. It was largely empty except for a few tourists like me snapping pictures of the war memorials, including tanks and missiles.

It was hard to believe so much time had passed since the Vietnam War. I was in the fourth grade when the brother of a classmate had returned to the United States after serving. We sat in the school auditorium and listened as he talked about what he experienced fighting our enemy, the North Vietnamese. Little did I know that one of my daughters would someday come from this far-away place. That day in a lunchroom auditorium with a couple of hundred other kids, I learned about war.

Joy's birthmother wasn't born until long after the fighting, and I wondered how much the North Vietnamese children knew about that part of their country's past. What propaganda were they told by the communist government? One thing I did know, each day the school kids, speaking fluent English, would besiege us to sell whatever they had, whether it was postcards, maps, books, or something I didn't want.

If not today, someday, because of the Western influence and

English language brought over by American soldiers, the school children would have the freedom to discover the truth for themselves. Perhaps in that way, we did win the war and our young men didn't die in vain.

Before we left Hanoi, I wanted to take Joy to see the puppet show, known locally as the Mua Roi Nuoc. After a few weeks with me, Joy wasn't as scared of people in her new environment and she was over the "hump" of visual stimulation evoking fear. I had heard good reviews from other adoptive families and Vietnamese locals who had seen the show.

It was different from other puppet plays I had seen or had put on in my church when I ran a puppet ministry. The puppet show reflected Vietnamese culture and history, and I was impressed with the visual creativity and esthetics. Though it was all in Vietnamese and I didn't understand the story line, the puppets were enchanting as they swayed to Vietnamese music played on traditional instruments. Joy watched attentively and seemed to enjoy the little marionettes as they danced rhythmically on the water stage.

Earlier in the week we were on our way to the camera store and Joy began singing when she heard music streaming out of one of the shops. I had sung Christmas carols to her at night when I put her to bed. The soft melodic tones helped to calm her spirit before drifting off to sleep. I continued to wonder how artistic she would be when she was older as I watched her enjoy the puppet show.

One nice thing about time is that it doesn't stop. At last, December 27 arrived, the day for the Giving and Receiving Ceremony. I dressed up in a black velvet dress and had bought a pretty outfit for Joy. The ceremony would take place in Thai Nguyen, about an hour and a half north of Hanoi.

Joy and I sat in the back of the van, and I held her in my arms as there were no car seats. On the way, we stopped and picked up a woman doctor that worked for Anne. She handed me an envelope that contained money to "help get the mother back on her feet." I did not ask any questions and did not open the envelope to see how much it contained.

I looked forward to once again seeing the countryside. After leaving downtown Hanoi, buildings were replaced with flat, luscious fields inundated with lots of small lakes. Eventually the flatness gave way to green rolling hills like the waves of the sea. Young Vietnamese women could be seen working in the flooded lands wearing the Non La, or Vietnamese hat. The hat is only worn in Vietnam and is made of leaves and bamboo. I had purchased two, one for Manisha and one for Joy as a souvenir, but left them on a plane somewhere between Vietnam and Florida.

We parked the van at the Department of Justice where the Giving and Receiving Ceremony would be held and walked inside. We were ushered into a small room where a short, elderly man, the equivalent to a court officer, sat us down. Joy's mother, Luu, walked in and took a seat to the right of us. Luu was teary-eyed and emotional as Joy rested quietly in my arms. When Luu reached for Joy to hold her one more time, she refused to go.

The ceremony began and the Court Officer glanced through the documents and asked us both some general questions.

"Is this what you want to do?"

I said, "Yes."

He asked Luu, "Is this what you want to do?"

She nodded.

It was all very official, and afterwards, he smiled, congratulated us, and offered to take our picture. I handed him my camera and he took two pictures of all of us standing beside a bust statue. A red Vietnamese flag with a yellow star hung limply to the back of us. Luu held a handkerchief in her hand which she used to dab her teary eyes.

After the ceremony we were dismissed to leave. As I followed Joy's birthmother down the steps outside the courthouse, I watched her walk away in a moment of personal reflection. She was returning to her life before Joy. With little prospect of better things for herself, she was willing to give her daughter that opportunity. I wished her good health and happiness as my life would be changed forever because she was brave. Joy would have hope of a wonderful future and a chance to live out her dreams.

In 1999, Vietnam had the highest abortion rate of any

country in the world.[8] Luu could have made the easy, selfish choice to end her baby's life. Nine years later as I pen these words, my eyes are full of tears as I picture what could have been and what happens every day across America. Suppose Luu had not been courageous. I never would have known Joy's contagious smile, her sweet hugs, her selfless love, her charming beauty, and her endless creativity. Most of all, Luu, through God's grace, gave me a priceless treasure and a pearl of great price.

A few years ago, I wrote a poem about Joy, and I dedicate it to Luu and all birthmothers who endure the pain and humiliation of bearing a baby out of wedlock; who choose life over death; sacrificial love over their own personal comfort; good over evil, and beauty over trash. May God use this poem to sear the conscience of those women who teeter on the verge of sorrow and regret. May they be as brave as Luu and make the heroic choice of letting their baby breathe, someday ride a bike, get married, and have children of their own. May they picture their "bundle of joy" chasing butterflies in a field of their own hopes and dreams. Through their courageous sacrifice and the gift of adoption, another woman's empty arms can be full of "joy."

---

[8] *The Christian Post*, March 31, 2008, "Vietnam Man Runs 'Abortion Orphanage,'" by Margie Mason, AP medical writer

My Joy

My Joy, my valentine, born in my heart,
My priceless treasure from a world apart.

My Joy, my daughter, who fills me with love,
May God richly bless you from his storehouse above,

My Joy who showers me with hugs and sweet things,
Pictures I cherish, who tells me her dreams

My Joy, a gymnast, a star in third grade,
My Joy, a sweet kiss and "I love you" each day.

My Joy, with little hands who fixes my hair when I'm hot,
My Joy, who forgives me when I blow up like a steam pot

My Joy, may you grow in God's love every year,
And each Valentine's day we always be nearer and dear,

My Joy, eat lots of chocolate, draw pictures and have fun,
For our journey together has only just begun

My Joy, my daughter, who I thought I would never see
I'll love you forever, you shall always be

My valentine wrapped in hugs and a kiss,
From your mom, our lazy cats, our loud dogs,
and your big sis.

Under Vietnamese law, Joy was legally my daughter. I
breathed a sigh of relief and enjoyed the trip back to Hanoi a lot
more than the trip to Thai Nguyen.

The hard part was ahead—leaving her behind.

184

Chapter Thirty

Do not let your hearts be troubled...

John 14:1

After we arrived back at the Lillie Hotel, I packed an overnight suitcase to go to the airport. We had to fly to Ho Chi Minh to drop Joy off with Anne. I would fly back to Hanoi and leave on December 30th. It would take two days to get back to Gainesville. I didn't want to be traveling on New Year's Eve.

When I purchased my airplane tickets, I had jokingly asked the Vietnamese Airlines attendant if they were flying on January 1.

"No," He said.

I asked, "Why not?"

"No customers."

I didn't want to be the first.

After time had gone so slowly over the past couple of weeks, the minutes became like a blur. In a matter of hours I would be leaving Vietnam. Joy had come so far in such a short amount of time. I was reminded of I John 4:18, that says "...perfect love drives out fear." Not that I had given her perfect love, but God in his mercy had made up the difference.

John 16:24 says, "Until now you have not asked for anything in my name. Ask and you will receive, and your joy will be complete."

As we waited at the airport for our flight, I reflected on my conversation with Mr. King earlier. Why had God allowed me to even know about the investigation of Anne? I had to take captive every thought as every cell in my body cried out to Him to bring Joy home. God had not abandoned Manisha in Nepal, and I knew He would take care of Joy. Although she would miss me for a time, as when Jesus left his disciples, He promised them that their grief would turn to joy (John 16:22).

We boarded the plane in the early evening to fly to Ho Chi Minh. North to south, Vietnam is 1,615 miles long and 375 miles at its widest point. To the east, it's bordered by Cambodia, Thailand, and Laos. Ho Chi Minh is located in the mid to southern part of Vietnam. As I peered out the window, I reflected back to when I flew to Nepal to adopt Manisha. Excited to be adopting my first daughter, I remembered looking down over the flat Vietnamese terrain on the way to Thailand. Little did I know then that just a few years later, I would be back adopting another little girl from Vietnam.

It was 709 miles to Ho Chi Minh, so the flight took only a couple of hours. We were served a traditional Vietnamese meal with chicken noodles that tasted even better than usual since it would save us from being hungry when we arrived. Joy settled in comfortably, and it was fun to watch her as her fear of new things had been replaced by a curiosity to explore.

She was seated to the right of me, her little legs just barely reaching to the front edge. I latched her seatbelt around her and, unlike Manisha, who gave me fits when I strapped her in, Joy was content to sit still. I lamented we weren't headed to Hong Kong instead of Southern Vietnam. After so many concerns about health issues—scabies, anemia, skin infections, autism, being small for her given age, and developmental delays, I began to appreciate even more how perceptive she was.

We arrived in Ho Chi Minh after dark and although we weren't able to see much, I could tell it was a lot different from Hanoi. A large city teaming with people, it churned with activity and brimmed with night life that was almost nonexistent in Hanoi. We took a taxi to the hotel, which was a little more upscale than the Lillie. With the Vietnamese adoption done, I felt a freedom I had not felt before. Sitting in a different hotel in new surroundings, I was excited—if only I didn't have to leave Joy the next day. She now easily went to bed and slept through the night without waking up crying.

The next morning, a taxi took us to Anne's home and in a brief downtown tour of Ho Chi Minh, I was surprised at how much it reminded me of America. Even more Western than Hanoi, it was a big metropolitan city full of people working, traveling, and enjoying life, a blend of Vietnamese culture and economic prosperity.

Was this not part of what the Vietnam War was about, to give the Vietnamese economic freedom and capitalism? Even today there isn't religious freedom, but that may soon come. Perhaps the best way to bring about freedom of religion is to provide people with a feeling of empowerment. Freedom in one area is contagious—it spills over into others.

After seeing a little bit of Ho Chi Minh, I was glad to have spent most of my time in Hanoi. If I had to be somewhere in Vietnam for a month, I would have chosen smaller and more conservative Hanoi over Ho Chi Minh.

The taxi dropped us off at Anne's home. Out front were tropical Vietnamese flowers and shade trees. The building was set back a few hundred feet from the main road, so it had a quiet, secluded feeling away from the street noise. When we walked in, we were greeted by one of her staff who took us to Anne's office.

I had never met Anne before. She was six feet tall, a rather large middle-aged woman, with on-going medical issues with her leg and needing a cane to get around. She sat at her desk in the middle of a spacious, rectangular room with a high ceiling. The desk was cluttered with papers and on the floor stood piles of folders. I wondered how she could find anything.

She rolled back from the desk and stopped her activity to talk with me about Joy. After a while, she told me about herself and how she came to be involved with adoptions in Vietnam. Her many stories reminded me of a cat with nine lives.

"By the way," she said, "A family in Gainesville, Texas will be here in March to adopt Thi My-Sa."

Before I could find out more, another adoptive family stopped by. Since they had some business they needed to discuss, I thanked Anne and got up to leave. As I walked outside to take in some fresh air, I met another adoptive parent with his little boy who was about three. We talked and shared our stories.

His new son was recovering from abdominal surgery and had a temporary colostomy. I was touched that he and his wife were willing to undertake the adoption of a child with such a serious medical condition. As he shared with me their adoption journey, he told me about a biological son of theirs who had the same malady. When they got word of this little boy, they knew he was meant to be their child. I heard similar stories from others in my brief stay at Anne's home. Does God not bring each child to the family that was meant for them?

There were several children that Anne was fostering, and she had also adopted a little Vietnamese girl that was four. Her daughter, Jade, took a liking to Joy and wanted to show us her bedroom. We followed her upstairs and she gave us a tour. Her room looked like any other American child's—brimming with Disney movies, books, and stuffed animals.

Afterwards we went back downstairs as Anne's staff had prepared lunch. Joy was clingy and wouldn't let me out of her sight. I think she feared I was going to leave. She would get excited playing with the other children and leave me, only to come running back to make sure I was still there. She had stacked her little suitcase beside mine to reassure herself I wasn't going anywhere without her. I hated the thought of leaving her in just a few hours.

One of the cooks came in and coaxed my daughter into another room to feed her. I knew this would be the best time to leave. I didn't want to let Joy know I was going as it would be too heartbreaking. I would have to slip away quietly. I remained silent without saying goodbye as the staff person carried her off into an adjoining room. I sat a little longer wishing I didn't have to go. I asked someone to make sure she was happy eating.

"She fine," she said. "She eating."

I thanked her and grabbed my suitcase, eyeing Joy's suitcase that now stood all alone beside her stroller. It would be a difficult three weeks until I saw her again. I walked slowly down the long hallway out front to wait on the taxi Anne had called for me, which showed up a few minutes later.

"I need to go to the airport," I told the driver. My heart was heavy as I prayed for Joy not to forget me during the time she would remain with Anne. I flew back to Hanoi and slept one last night at the Lillie Hotel, missing Joy immensely. The room was so quiet and lonely without her. Wondering what she was doing, I called to see how she was.

"She is fine," Anne assured me. "She cried a little when she realized you were gone, but she's okay now." I wondered if she told me the truth or if she just said that to make me feel better. Knowing Joy, I was sure she cried a lot.

The next morning I paid the hotel bill and finished packing all my suitcases to leave. It was amazing the clutter I had managed to accumulate that I didn't want to take home—half-eaten bags of food, diapers that wouldn't fit in the suitcase, Christmas decorations that weren't worth saving, and toys that Joy had already lost interest in. After feeling at times like a prisoner stuck in Hanoi over Christmas, my time in Vietnam was coming to an end. The next morning I said my goodbyes to the folks at the hotel; the lady in the "dungeon" who, according to Jenni, made the best Jasmine tea on the planet, and the lady at the front desk who had been so kind.

"Please thank Jenni again for the stuffed animals," the receptionist told me. One afternoon before Jenni left to return home, my sensitive, young traveling partner had emptied her backpack on the counter and several beloved stuffed animals tumbled out. She had planned to take them to an orphanage, but when she found out how needy the young lady's children were, she decided to give them to her. It was a touching moment as the receptionist received them from her.

I took a taxi to the airport and boarded the flight back to Hong Kong. Unlike when I left Kathmandu several years earlier, leaving Hanoi was uneventful. As the plane took off and flew over the city, I looked down at the streets and buildings receding beneath me that had been my home for the last four weeks. January 1st, 2000, would soon be upon us, ushering in a new century and millennium full of hope and promise.

I was glad to be on my way back to Gainesville, but part of my heart would remain behind as I thought about my "Bundle of Joy" in Ho Chi Minh. But only for a time—I believed God would bring Joy to me because God loved Joy more than I did. She needed a "forever" home and I needed a "forever" little girl from Vietnam, the second of my "Children of Dreams."

Faith is refusing to give up, believing in dreams not yet seen, and knowing God gives us both. Hope had already arrived and Joy was on the way. The days till January 25 would pass quickly. I began to think about all the things I needed to buy, like a baby crib, a high chair, diapers.... I couldn't wait!

Chapter Thirty-One

Wednesday, January 26, 2000, 5:30 p.m.

He settles the barren woman in her home as a happy mother of children

Psalm 113:9

East Coast storm paralyzes airports, roads, rails
January 25, 2000

From staff and wire reports

(CNN) ... Heavy snow and strong winds in the eastern United States put the freeze on travelers around the country Tuesday, with blizzard-like conditions closing airports from North Carolina northward and causing significant delays and cancellations of flights into and out of the region... New York's LaGuardia and Philadelphia International Airport were completely closed. Very few flights took off or landed at JFK and Newark airports, the Port Authority of New York and New Jersey said.[9]

My conflicted feelings wouldn't be erased until Joy landed safely on the ground in Jacksonville. Anticipation, worry,

---

[9] CNN.com, January 25, 2000

frustration, fear, hope, and joy wrapped up in one. How the human heart can contain so many emotions at once is baffling. Surely the jars of clay we live in weren't made for such spiritual beings as we are. Words too limiting to express my emotions, I sat glued to my television screen watching the scene unfold where runways were shut down due to the massive snowstorm. The adoption agency had phoned to tell me that Anne's flight had been delayed leaving New York because of the blizzard. Anne had another little girl named Amber that she was escorting to a family in the Newark area. Anne, her daughter, and Joy wouldn't arrive until Wednesday, January 26, around 9:30 p.m. It had been one more unexpected delay and one more day to worry had I let my emotions run rampant.

The last three weeks since flying home from Vietnam had seemed surreal. Nothing extraordinary happened when the clock struck midnight on January 1, 2000, marking the beginning of the new millennium. Once the initial worry of a global crisis passed, I crammed as much math and reading into the hours as I could so I wouldn't feel guilty after Joy arrived and Manisha and I skipped homeschooling for a few days. Joy's room was decorated and made ready with a borrowed crib from the Murphys. I had purchased everything I thought I would need, including a car seat, high chair, diapers, and a diaper changing pad, and hoped I wasn't forgetting anything important. Joy would be my first and only baby because Manisha wasn't a baby when I adopted her.

Having such a young one in diapers, single parenting, homeschooling, and working full time seemed daunting, but is this not what I had chosen? I reminded myself that as hard as things might seem in the beginning, no child ever went to college wearing diapers. Mine certainly wouldn't be the first.

I had made numerous phone calls to Vietnam in the previous three weeks to Mr. King at the U.S. Embassy on the progress of Joy's adoption. Each day was a step in faith that God would bring her to me. With the beginning of the new millennium, I imagined a new beginning for the three of us as a "forever family" brought together through God's providence and love. I longed for children years earlier when I was married and couldn't get pregnant. Memories of a distant past that no longer held me captive, chains

192

loosened from the emotions that bled of hurt and betrayal.

Forgiveness had helped me to let go and embrace God's love. I hoped God would give me the grace to run the race set before me with perseverance. Single parenting to one child can be overwhelming. Did I really know what I was getting myself into? I am sure Mary, the mother of Jesus, must have felt the same when she found herself with child under dubious circumstances, but she never questioned God and rejoiced over the baby within her womb. The feeling had never left me that there was something missing before Joy. I knew I was supposed to have two children. Now our family would be complete the way God intended.

"Are you ready to go, Manisha?

"I am coming, Mommy," she called from her room.

I grabbed her coat and pulled my black and red Mexican-looking shawl over my head. Even when it was freezing, I hated coats. It was due to hit the 30s later in the evening. I wondered if Joy would be warmly dressed coming from the cold in New York City. I tucked Joy's coat that I had bought her in Vietnam inside the diaper bag just in case she needed it.

Wednesday night, Thursday, and Friday would be my only days off from captioning since I had missed a month of work while in Vietnam. I lamented I couldn't be rich for two weeks so I could have more time to prepare for the adjustment after Joy's arrival. I forced myself to look at the bright side of things. I worked at home and didn't have to leave the house to earn a paycheck.

I gave Manisha a quick hug. "Are you ready to meet your new baby sister?" I asked her excitedly.

"Yes," she said emphatically. "Let's go."

Curtis Murphy would be arriving a little after us at the airport. We had arranged for him to come in his car because Anne and her daughter needed transportation back to Gainesville where her mother lived. It was just providence that we lived in the same town. My red Firebird could only hold four people, one too many to fit in my sports car. We would meet him at the airport a couple of hours later since we were leaving Gainesville early.

The hour and a half trip in the car was one of anticipation and nervousness. I couldn't wait for Manisha and Joy to meet. I had dreamed about this day for more than three years, even before I began the adoption process. It was important to me that Manisha have a sister, someone that would be family to her when I was no longer around. Now that the moment was finally here, it seemed dream-like.

I inserted one of the Focus on the Family *Adventures in Odyssey* tapes into the tape player and cranked on the heat. Manisha had worn her bright red flannel outfit which could serve as clothes or pajamas. Who knew what time we would return to Gainesville, particularly if the plane was late.

I reflected back to a few weeks earlier when I came home from Vietnam. Manisha had seemed so big after spending a month with Joy. Seven and half years apart in age might seem like a lot now, but I knew down the road, those years wouldn't matter as they reached maturity. I was one month shy of nine when Paige, my sister, was born. Manisha would be nine on February 23.

I was glad Joy wasn't a newborn—someone once told me that the only things newborns do are eat, sleep and poop. In hindsight, fifteen months seemed like a perfect age to adopt a second child. Young enough for bonding with an older sibling yet not so young that Manisha couldn't help me. Manisha didn't see it that way, though. She saw Joy as an instant playmate. I hoped that wouldn't change.

It was almost dark now that the sun had receded behind some clouds to the west of us. As I sped along I-10 east toward Jacksonville, I had a few more moments to reflect before pulling into the parking lot at the airport.

Would Joy remember me after almost a month? I wondered if Manisha would have pangs of jealousy having been the center of my attention since I adopted her almost six years earlier. Would she remain seizure-free? That was a big one. I had received the final medical report back from Dr. Hostetter on

Manisha's blood work. She had sent a sample of her blood to the Centers for Disease Control in Atlanta for testing with a new, more sensitive test for neurocysticercosis. The doctors had been unable to confirm the diagnosis which made the test results disappointing. Either Manisha didn't have neurocysticercosis or the test wasn't as sensitive as they had hoped. I knew in all these things I had to trust God, but if my mind was left to wonder, it always seemed to return to Manisha's haunting medical history.

I looked at my watch and it was 7:00 p.m. I felt my stomach grumbling from hunger as I had been too anxious to eat before we left. The tape was close to finishing as we approached Jacksonville. Too excited to sleep, it had kept Manisha awake but quiet on the way.

I had shared with her about my time in Vietnam and what Joy was like to prepare her. Thinking about the two of them together made me think back to my own childhood. One of my favorite memories was when I was nine and my sister was born. I remembered going to the hospital and looking through the glass window at all the babies and the nurse pointing to which one was my new baby sister. How excited I was as I stood and admired her scrunched-up face and whiffs of hair. I remembered when we brought her home from the hospital how I wasn't jealous but our dog, Gypsy, was. She hid in the corner for a week and wouldn't have anything to do with anybody.

When I was eleven my younger brother, Thomas, was born, and although I was happy to have a brother also, I was more jealous of him than I ever was of Paige. He got away with murder. Okay, maybe not murder, but it seemed like it when he took little bites out of all my favorite pieces of candy hidden in my room and nobody did anything about it.

In the end, we all grew up loving each other and have a good relationship today. Both of them are married and have children of their own. Not only would Joy and Manisha have each other, they already had cousins and extended family which I never had. When the time seemed right after Joy's initial adjustment, we would travel to Atlanta so everyone could meet her.

At last we arrived at the Jacksonville Airport and I parked in the well-lit, enclosed parking area which I deemed safer than the dark outdoor lot. It would also require less walking for Anne with her wobbly knee. As I turned off the car, Manisha put on her shoes and waited impatiently for me to open the door. As I did so, a cold rush of air chilled my exposed skin. I couldn't believe how much the temperature had dropped in the last hour and a half.

"Make sure you put your coat on."

"Okay, Mommy," she replied.

We walked to the connecting overhead bridge from the parking lot to the terminal, and I found the kiosk which displayed the arrivals and departures. I checked the arrival time and gate for Joy's flight which showed it would be thirty minutes late. We would have plenty of time to grab something to eat.

"How long till Joy gets here?" Manisha asked.

"If it's 7:30 p.m. now and she arrives at 9:30 p.m., how much time will pass?"

She hated it when I asked her "time" questions, but I always made use of opportunities when they presented themselves.

"I don't know," she answered.

"It will be about two hours." I wasn't going to press her on it tonight. There would be other opportunities. The hard part would be to keep her entertained while we waited.

The Jacksonville Airport was not that big, and at this time of night, not that busy. We found a place to eat that had a television and claimed the two best seats—right in front of the screen, to pass the time while we waited. Curtis had called and said he would arrive around 9:00 p.m.

The weather report showed snowplows removing mounds of debris from roads in several cities in the Northeast. I couldn't believe Joy had arrived in the middle of a huge blizzard. One airplane had run off the runway in New York and I had panicked that it was hers. The last couple of hours of waiting seemed the longest.

As the minutes grudgingly ticked away, I watched as a couple of other planes came in, releasing passengers in one fell swoop of instant noise and controlled confusion that slowly dispersed into quietness. At last the time drew near as Curtis walked up and found us waiting by the arrival gate.

"How is everybody doing?" He asked.

"The plane is running about thirty minutes late."

Manisha wanted to walk around so the two of them took off leaving me alone. I took another sip of my Coke as I watched the captions on the television screen. *Not bad,* I thought to myself. I wondered if I knew the captioner. CNN was captioned by Vitac, one of NCI's competitors. Too bad they didn't have Fox News on. Every Monday night, 9:00 to 11:00 p.m. I would caption "Hannity and Colmes" and "On the Record" with Greta Van Susteren. I checked my time. "Hannity and Colmes" was on, but the plane would be here soon, about 9:45 p.m., and my thoughts focused on Joy.

Shortly Curtis and Manisha returned as the overhead sign lit up that the plane from Newark, New Jersey, was approaching. I stood up and walked over to peer out the dark window. A few minutes later a large jet cautiously approached its resting spot. The airport employees pulled the portable gangplank up to the plane and latched it to the plane's side. Soon people began to pour through the open doors. Curtis, Manisha and I stood and waited, looking for a large woman, one Vietnamese child, and a baby to appear. The plane must have been completely full as huge numbers of passengers exited. Humanity kept pouring through the doors as I excitedly waited in anticipation. The mass exodus slowed down to a trickle and there was still no sign of them.

"I wondered if they missed the plane," I mused to myself, afraid to say anything out loud. We waited another minute and no one else exited through the doors. I double checked the flight number and date. Did I make a mistake? I had almost given up hope they were on the plane when there appeared through the doorway a heavy set woman precariously walking with a cane, pushing Joy in a stroller, and one little girl, Jade, her daughter, following closely behind.

"There they are," I shouted, stating the obvious. I should have known Anne would be the last person off the plane because of her leg. We hurriedly walked over to them. Exhausted, Anne looked relieved to see me. I could tell the last few days had been an ordeal.

"Joy did great," she said, "mostly sleeping."

I squatted down to eye level in front of Joy's stroller.

"Do you remember me?" I asked her.

She looked at me questioningly, as if to say, "Why did you leave me in Vietnam?" *Someday I would explain it all*, I thought to myself, and reached over and gave her a big hug.

"I want to push her," Manisha insisted.

Anne was more than willing to relinquish responsibility of Joy to her new big sister. As Manisha grabbed the handlebars of the stroller, I quickly stepped back a few feet to take a picture.

"Smile." The camera responded with a click as I snapped the first picture of my two daughters together.

"Can I hold her?" Manisha asked.

I walked back over to Joy and unsnapped the safety belt around her waist. She was holding her favorite toy I had left with her, a little round yellow rattle with a fake mirror on the inside. I lifted her out of the stroller and handed her to Manisha. Joy stared at the new person whom she had never met. Looking tired from her journey, she seemed content to let things take their course.

Manisha walked around proudly holding Joy on her hip and giving her a peck on the forehead. I was thankful that she had so much love to give her. Manisha was happy to hold her new sister, and it gave me a few minutes to sit and talk to Anne.

Curtis had walked off to check on the progress of the luggage, and Jade, who seemed to have been overlooked during the arrival, stood by holding several bags which she gladly set down beside us. Anne handed me some paperwork, including Joy's passport and adoption papers. I would have to sort through them later. I sat beside Anne on the bench as we watched Manisha and Joy together.

"What is this?" I asked, as I peered into the bags Jade had discarded. In one was an adult-sized yellow sweatshirt.

"It was so cold in the New York airport and I had no warm clothes for Joy," Anne said. "A man saw her shivering and took his shirt off and put it on her."

I held up the yellow sweatshirt and wondered who the man was. I would never be able to thank him personally, but God knew.

"Isn't it interesting, as young as Manisha is, that she knows to poke her hip out to hold her," Anne commented.

"Yes," I responded, "just like she's an old pro at it."

As we sat and rested, I contemplated the future, enjoying the scene of Joy and Manisha getting to know each other. There had only been a few times this side of paradise that seemed perfect and this was one of those blissful moments. I realized at that moment that God brought Joy to me and not any other child.

My first referral had hepatitis and God had not given me peace to adopt her. The second referral, Thi My-Sa, was my child of prayer, but unable to be adopted by me because of paperwork. The third, Nguyen Thi My-Duyen, disappeared before I ever arrived in Vietnam, and finally, Joy.

I knew I was where I was supposed to be. Nothing had happened by accident, mistake, or coincidence. The past and the future receded into the background as I watched my two daughters together for the first time—a memory that would be stored in my treasure chest of God's blessings.

As Manisha continued to walk around with Joy nestled securely on her hip, I paused to reflect on another moment, one in the distant future. Would it not be that different when we arrived in heaven? Jesus would welcome us with scarred hands, embracing us with His perfect love. We would know we were His, bought with a price, our adoption papers sealed forever. What a reunion that would be when we truly arrived "home." This night was a foretaste of an even more perfect reunion, a symbol of what God has in store for all of us.

God had unleashed the chains of bondage to sin and healed me from the past. His grace had helped me to overcome my fears and given me strength in weariness. Only through His miracles had insurmountable obstacles been overcome. He had made what seemed impossible possible. Through all the storms, trials, and tribulations, He had vanquished the powers of deceit and deception. God answered my prayers, redeemed by His unfathomable love, by making me a mother to two orphaned children. He gave me a treasure hidden in a field and a pearl of great price. Through adoption I was able to create my family as God had given me my Children of Dreams.

Bits and Pieces

In the beginning...

Genesis 1:1

Although I grew up in a moral home, it was not a Christian home. As a young teen, I read the Bible in the darkness of my room under covers and was amazed at the humanity of Jesus Christ and His unrelenting love for those who hated him. It was as if I was among the masses that listened to Him on the hills of Jerusalem. I was amazed by His teachings and accepted His salvation—so I could be with Him in heaven for all eternity. I didn't want to go to hell.

Without a Christian worldview, my choices were based on human determination and not godly wisdom. Neil Armstrong's words when he stepped on the moon, "That's one small step for man, one giant leap for mankind," resonated with my "nothing ventured, nothing gained" mentality. I believed I could "go where no man [or woman] had gone before," as the Enterprise did in the original *Star Trek* series. Whether it was chasing aliens on distant planets or becoming the next Jacques Cousteau, I thought if I made straight A's and met "Mr. Right," my dreams would come true. They didn't.

In the fall of 1985, I was a full-time student at the University of Florida when I returned home from school one day and discovered that my husband had packed his bags and left. I frantically called him to see where he was. Why wasn't he coming home? Did he not love me anymore?

After working six years as a court reporter putting him through graduate and medical school, he had promised me that I could return to school when he began his residency in radiation oncology. Obtaining my college degree was another "dream" that had been taken from me. Now all that mattered was my husband had left. I withdrew from college for the semester to deal with the crisis. We had a few counseling sessions, but he wasn't willing to work on the marriage. I continued to work on me.

The following January, I enrolled at Santa Fe College to retake the Calculus course I had dropped the previous fall. When I got to derivatives, a mental flashback to my husband abandoning me made it seem insurmountable. The professor had been covering derivatives the day I came home and discovered he was gone. Rather than dropping the course or communicating with my professor at Santa Fe College, I quit going. Despite attempts by my instructor to contact me, I never answered her calls. I received an "F" for the course on my otherwise impeccable record at Santa Fe College.

A few years later, when the divorce was final and God had given me new direction, an opportunity arose through the National Court Reporters Association to enroll in the External Degree Program at the University of Alabama. The thought of earning that elusive college degree consumed me. Without missing a beat, I called the University of Alabama to obtain more information on applying to the program.

Suddenly that "F" in Calculus looked "damning" on my record. I had no one to blame except myself. I deserved the "F." There was nothing I could do to change it. The ink had long dried, recorded in the books for all to see, including the Registrar's Office at the University of Alabama.

I went to the Office of Student Affairs at Santa Fe College to obtain a copy of my transcript. Thirteen "A's" and one "F" were printed across my transcript. I shared with the counselor the circumstances surrounding the "F", lamenting how I wished I had dealt with it and how I hated seeing it on my permanent record. It never occurred to me that they could do anything about it. I asked her if she thought it would cause my application to be rejected from the University of Alabama.

The counselor told me to wait in her office for a few minutes and she would be right back. She left and returned shortly and handed me two sheets of paper. The first sheet contained my official transcript. On the second page, in large letters written across the Calculus I course were the words, *No Record.*

Santa Fe College had deleted the Calculus I class from their computers. As far as they were concerned, I never took the course. There was "no record." I looked at the transcript page, and sure enough, Calculus I was not there. I didn't know colleges had it in their power to remove courses that students had taken and received failing grades.

That day God showed me forgiveness. I left knowing I didn't deserve that kind of mercy. I realized God had revealed to me a greater truth. I had to forgive everybody that I had any bitterness toward if I wanted to receive God's forgiveness. The day marked a turning point in my life. I knew I was without excuse.

I couldn't just forgive once—it had to become a way of life. How could I be a good mother if I brought all of that baggage into a "forever" family with Manisha and Joy? Forgiveness was the cornerstone of my healing and essential for God's redemption.

It wasn't until after my painful divorce that I understood it is God who shapes our dreams and directs our paths. It was then that I gave all of my life to Jesus Christ—including my dreams. Little did I know what wonderful plans God had in store. Not that my life has been easy; if we embrace a radical Christianity, I don't think it will be. God took me as I was—bitter, hurt, and angry—and began a huge reconstruction project.

One hot afternoon when I arrived at my favorite pool to take a cool dip, a group of swimmers were already there with an assortment of things, including tanks, snorkels, flippers, face masks, and unusual, intimidating gadgets that I came to know later as octopuses and BCs. I jumped at the opportunity to learn how to scuba dive.

I could not have known then how God would use such an amazing pastime for His divine purposes. God had a plan to prepare me to be a single mother—He wanted to equip me to rescue two children from the remotest regions of the earth.

I was mesmerized by the unparalleled beauty of the waters of the deep. With unlimited visibility, air becomes blue, sand glistens like snow, eels mimic wavy stems of plants, and blue

202

rays glide like a flock of birds. The high-definition, Blu-ray cinematography created a world of enchantment dotted with multi-colored coral, sea anemones, blue damsels, and grouper. If I was lucky, the occasional eel and nurse shark would reward me with a surprise appearance.

I often wondered why God would create an underwater world with so much diversity that most would never experience. I never felt closer to God than when swimming weightlessly in the ocean's depths, feeling His presence in every breath inhaled through my regulator. I had indeed met the Great Master, who cares for the simplest of creatures—even the little worm I discovered clinging to a sunken ship at fifty feet on a night dive. Never would I doubt that God was the Creator.

My dives throughout the world gave me allegorical clues to the great battle waged in the unseen world of good versus evil. The immediate dangers that lurked in the deep became metaphors to me for human sin and evil.

On a more practical level, Scuba diving helped me to develop self-esteem, overcome insecurity, face my fear of failure, and deal with not always being physically comfortable. I have some pretty tall tales I could tell.

Without God's work in my heart on so many different levels, I would have remained a miserable, wretched, person—codependent and insecure. I cringe when I think what I would have missed out on if God had not had mercy on me, but God promises to heal the brokenhearted and restore what the locusts have eaten.

God brought me through many adventures that became life lessons, more than enough to last a lifetime, but it was during the years in the "wilderness" before I left for Nepal, while in the crucible of suffering, that God did His greatest work on my heart. I realized, sitting in a chair at the Jacksonville Airport that cold night, it was only through forgiveness that God was able to fulfill my dreams, redeemed by His grace and mercy.

…choose for yourselves this day whom you will serve…

Joshua 24:15

How are my daughters doing today? This was the most common question asked by the proofreaders of the first draft of my book. As I put the finishing touches on *Children of Dreams,* I can't believe how quickly the years have slipped away. We have our children for just a short season. One day we turn around and our babies and toddlers are headed to school with backpacks and a lunchbox. We barely blink and they want the keys to our car. I hope the wedding bells and nursery are still a few years away.

Manisha Hope, my oldest, will be eighteen in just a few months. She would have died when she was seven if I had not adopted her. She would never have known the Lord, never felt a mother's love, or had a chance to become everything God created her to be.

Joy would have remained in the northern reaches of Vietnam without the opportunity to achieve her creative potential, to know Jesus personally, and to fill my heart with so much love. I would have spent the rest of my life never knowing the child God had chosen for me. Our Lord doesn't put any child with any parent. There is a great plan crafted by our heavenly Father from the beginning of time.

As much as I would like to think my children are mine, they aren't. They belong to God and I do not own them. They are on loan to me to raise and love for a few short years, painfully fleeting as I look back, but hopefully, when the Lord returns, He will say to me, "Well done, my good and faithful servant."

Now that Manisha is almost an adult, I have been reflecting on what words of wisdom I will impart to her as she approaches adulthood. She will soon be stepping out into the world on her own, and I wonder whether I have done enough to prepare her for the harsh realities of life.

In so many ways I know I have failed because I am not

prefect. We have all failed and come up wanting. But God loves Manisha and Joy more than I do, and I know my prayer and my heart's desire, above all else, for both of my girls, is to love the Lord with all their hearts. Ultimately, they will have to choose which road they will travel and which God they will serve—the God of the Bible, or a manmade god that could entice them away from everything I have tried to teach them and show them.

God was the perfect parent and Adam and Eve disobeyed Him. If the perfect Father can have rebellious children, it doesn't make me a bad parent if my children go up against everything I believe. Part of letting go is allowing them to choose how they will live and accepting them as they are, whether I agree with their lifestyle or not. I must love them anyway. God is our example. Help me, Lord Jesus, to be like You.

Some of the saddest stories I have heard are from adoptive parents whose children have chosen the wrong friends, made incredibly foolish choices, squandered amazing opportunities, or refused to acknowledge Jesus as their personal Savior. Often times the parents blame themselves for their children's mistakes.

Hopefully, in twenty years God can write HiStory, the testimony of two orphans who faithfully served Him, whether Manisha becomes a missionary, Joy a doctor, or they are "ordinary" in the eyes of the world but "heroes" to someone in need. For now, that part of the story must wait. At seventeen and ten, my daughters have barely begun to live, but God has given them the opportunity through adoption to become everything they were created to be. I hope as they both mature, they will dream big dreams, climb huge mountains, and continue to walk humbly with their God.

My treasure hidden in the mountains of Nepal, it seems like yesterday when Manisha and I first met and walked around the building picking flowers and admiring the birds. She is almost eighteen and the biggest issue we "fight over" is why I will not buy her a car. She is a beautiful young woman who has accepted Jesus as her Savior, and there is evidence of her relationship with Him in her life. Friends call her the "little mother," because she has been such a wonderful big sister to Joy (most of the time) for which I am thankful.

Getting through the teenage years with my oldest daughter has not been easy. We still have a couple of more years to go, and I pray that God will be with her each day, draw her unto Himself, and keep her safe. There is no room for pride when raising a teenager; it has been hard work but rewarding.

As an aside, Manisha's Algebra teacher this semester is the same professor that gave me the "F" and for which Santa Fe College removed the failing grade from my record—the object lesson God used to teach me the meaning of forgiveness. What would I have thought twenty-three years ago if I had known that someday that same professor would be my daughter's instructor?

Joy just turned ten and is now in fifth grade. It's been eight years since I was in Vietnam. My pearl of great price—how empty my life would have been without the one I almost didn't get. I have been homeschooling Joy for the past two years and I try to make it a lifestyle and not a drudgery (most of the time). We bought seasonal passes to Disney World for a year and have made several trips to study the African animals, learn about wildlife, and develop a greater awareness of history through the elaborate exhibits. At Epcot, the World Showcase, I have introduced Joy to other cultures from around the world, and we've eaten at several of the restaurants offering French, German, and Moroccan cuisine.

Soon we will go on a kayaking trip to Atsena Otie Island off the coast of Cedar Key to study migratory birds and the history of the island. I have used homeschooling as an excuse to have fun and learn about God's great universe, where His handiwork is revealed in the precious life and beauty around us.

Joy is also a talented gymnast on the girls' gymnastics team and will compete at level seven in January. If she stays injury-free and I can afford it, she has the physical agility and strength to go as far with it as she wants.

She received Jesus into her heart when she was young and asks many questions—she is my deep thinker and shallow thinker, my creative one and challenging one. Give her paper and pencil and she's happy. I learned early on how much she loved to draw when walls had scribbles that appeared from nowhere and books had marks that I knew weren't "copyrighted." Her love notes have inspired me to someday make a book of "Love Notes to Mom." I wish there were a way I could bottle up her creativity and sell it. I could make a fortune. With great creativity and talent come great challenges. I am sure my hair will be a beautiful shade of silvery gray by the time I get her through the teenage years.

I wouldn't trade my children for anything in the world (although they might trade me in for a younger version because, in their words, "you are old"). As God's precious gifts, I am amazed, especially now that I wrote *Children of Dreams,* how God did what was humanly impossible—without an awesome God, I wouldn't have either of my daughters!

Parenting is the hardest job in the world. Imperfect and full of flaws, my ability to be a single parent has been harder than anything I could have imagined. My kids could give plenty of examples of all my foibles, but love covers a multitude of sins, fortunately.

I never set out to be a homeschooling mom. It just happened because both my children do so much better academically with one-on-one teaching, as shown by the Iowa Skills test scores each year. But my main goal has been to give my children a Christian worldview. If I accomplish that, I feel my most important objective will have been reached and the academic achievement will be gravy.

My favorite line for "keeping on" is something I heard a few years ago at the Homeschooling Convention in Orlando: The worst day homeschooling is better than the best day in public or private school. I have done all three and truly believe it.

Both my daughters would receive an "A plus" in Americanism. I did westernize Manisha after all my worries to the contrary. They have adjusted well to growing up in a single-parent family (they don't know anything different, unlike children from divorce). As far as I know, they have never experienced any prejudice. I don't even think Joy would know what it means. On the surface, an outsider would never know the depravity from which they came.

——— —— ——

...I am the Lord who heals you

Exodus 15:26

Praise the Lord that Manisha has been off seizure medicine for six years and hasn't had a seizure in eight years. Hopefully neurocysticercosis will never raise its ugly head again. As I told the insurance company, the parasite died and can't come back to life. Good riddance!

He will respond to the prayer of the destitute

Psalm 102:17

There was one bit of unfinished business that haunted me. It was so deep I never shared it with anyone because I didn't think anyone would understand. In some ways I couldn't understand, except in quiet moments, light, wispy thoughts would drift into my consciousness from the past, dream-like, from deep within my soul. Just like the little dog, Fifi, that many years ago I rescued, I wanted to know that the little girl, Thi My-Sa, whom I prayed about for so long, was happy and loved. The image of her sitting in what looked like a steel cage with bars never left me even after I came home with Joy. I never got over the fact that I had left her there with an uncertain future.

Even when Anne mentioned to me in passing, while I was at her home in Ho Chi Minh, that she was being adopted in March, I struggled emotionally, for I felt that I had let her down. I had prayed concerning Thi My-Sa for months after she was found in a store being beaten by somebody that was not her mother and taken away to the orphanage by strangers. I wanted to ask Anne more, but every time I tried, something prevented me from finding out anything. Perhaps Anne was unwilling to talk about it, but I had loved this little girl that had such a difficult beginning.

I was glad she was eventually adopted, but there are always the "what if's"? Suppose I had waited just a little bit longer? I knew that Joy was supposed to be my daughter, so why did I have such a hard time letting go of Thi My-Sa? Could it be that my prayers were meant to "keep her," like I had kept Fifi many years earlier until her new master arrived? Maybe my prayers had protected her, given her a chance, even as she waited month after month.

Several months after Joy arrived home from Vietnam, Jackie, the adoptive mother from Canada, whom I had met in Hanoi, emailed me asking if the person who had adopted Thi My-Sa could contact me. She knew someone that knew her, and through the grapevine of Vietnamese adoptive parents, had somehow tracked me down. I wondered, could this be God's way, in His mercy, of bringing me closure? Of letting me know that Thi My-Sa was loved, was being raised in a Godly home, and that my prayers had made a difference? Could I be sure I had done the right thing in relinquishing her and not feel guilty about it?

I knew Anne would never tell me the name of the family or give me their contact information. Anyway, who would understand how I felt? I had my two children, so what difference would it make? It made a difference in my soul. Once you have a place in your heart for a person, that spot belongs to them, whether it's a child, a friend, or a mentor. No other child can replace that child. Every child has her "special place."

When I received the email from Jackie, I was stunned. Strangely enough, they lived in Gainesville, Texas. I was thrilled to think the family wanted to contact me, but reluctant to think it would ever happen. I didn't want to get my hopes up. After all that I had been through, I didn't want to be disappointed.

I will let Kris speak here as she says so well how God in His mercy called her to get in touch with me:

I said to Anne, "Well, Joy is the name I want to name her."

Anne laughed. "That is a coincidence. The lady who was going to adopt her named her daughter that she adopted Joy."

I said, "A coincidence?"

She said, "Well, she was destined for Gainesville, but not Florida—Texas."

I asked her for your email or address, and she wasn't forthcoming, pleading disorganization. She didn't want us to get together, for Abbey had two different sets of documents and was two people. The birth certificate you had put her three months older than the one I had, with two different names.

Interesting.

I was compelled to find you.

I knew I had to find you.

I knew in my heart you hurt from it, at least then.

I had to see you. I had to show you.

I had to let you know she was happy with us.

I knew instinctively you were like me, and when you could find her happy, any leftover feelings would dissipate.

I knew when we drove thru Gainesville the first Christmas and I didn't know how to reach you [by phone], I grieved for you.

For me. For her.

I knew she had to make that connection.

I felt empty for the whole trip, for you to be with us for a brief time.

For you to see us. For us to see you.

For her to know that she had people pulling for her, even if she was never to know her bio mom.

When we were invited back to Orlando the second Christmas by our-brother-in-law, he paid for our trip and motel. I told Kirk, "We have to meet her."

He understood as a man would, but I felt it deeply. He goes along with what I think is right, as he did to see her Dong Nai Orphanage and the market where she was found and abandoned. Now she talks about it quite often.

It was the right thing to do in both instances, because with the orphanage, the director had gone home, and he drove back in to see her and hug her. We took pictures of him and his wife. It was a God thing. Like meeting you.

I still have the papers you sent me somewhere in Abbey's file. I want her to know her whole story, because only then can she honestly resolve it.

I emailed you a couple of years ago[10] and asked you if Abbey and I alone could come and visit you, and you never responded. It hurt me a little. I thought, *well, maybe you have a boyfriend, a live-in or maybe you don't want to clean house,* or some random thoughts. *Maybe you didn't like me.*

I just let it go. I thought, *well, maybe you didn't get my email.* I just thought, *there is this connection,* and Abbey and I talk about you. She has a place in her heart for you, because she knows when she was too little to understand or control anything, you were praying for her.

She has a love for the thought of you.

I wanted her to have a knowledge of who you were, and a trip, or a halfway meeting someday, would be so good for her (and you), and your two daughters... we would probably not have her had you not held onto her until you couldn't any longer, and had you not been there to pray for her constantly.

Love, Kris

---

[10] Kris contacted me by email initially, but I didn't receive her email on their first trip to Florida. It wasn't until another year had passed, when she emailed me a second time that they were passing through Gainesville that we met.

Every child is a precious gift from God. Some of us are called to give birth. Some of us are called to adopt. Sometimes our role is to pray and intercede for those who can't speak for themselves. Sometimes we are called to sponsor children in Third World countries. If we all do our part, we can make a difference in the life of a child. God knows the beginning and the end. We can rest assured His plan is perfect.

Abbey and I did meet, and Kris and I shared a few special moments as we watched Joy and Abbey play together. I could now have complete peace and assurance that I had done exactly what God had called me to do; in His infinite wisdom He gave me Joy. But before Joy, He had given me the high calling of praying for Abbey for an entire year so she could be adopted by Kris and her dear husband. Abbey was their first daughter following six boys, and very much wanted and loved.

Even in today's fallen world, there are flawless pictures that create perfection, if only for a fleeting moment, but we grab hold of them knowing they are a foretaste of the heaven that awaits us, where there will be no more beatings and cries of the destitute, where God will heal every bruise and wipe every tear. I hope to see Abbey and Kris again next year in February when we travel to San Antonio for one of Joy's gymnastics meets. God continues to work out ways for our paths to cross and for that I am thankful.[11]

…and the truth shall make you free

John 8:32

---

[11] See pictures at back of book

One thing I look forward to when I get to heaven is learning the truth about things I will probably never know here. I will never forget the feeling I had when I arrived in Vietnam and was told the baby I was adopting was "kidnapped."

Eight years later, after someone came up to me and asked, "What happened to the baby that was kidnapped?" I realized I couldn't gloss over things. I needed to delve into what happened so the truth could set free my frozen emotions. I didn't want to reveal that part of what I experienced because it was so painful, but those who read my story wanted to know everything.

There are many warnings in *Children of Dreams* for would-be adoptive parents—beware of who you work with and bathe your hopes and dreams in prayer to the only wise God who is all-knowing and all-powerful, "… for the battle is not yours, but God's" (2 Chronicles 20:15).

Since being asked the question about the little girl who was kidnapped, I prayed and fasted, and this is what God has led me to believe. I can't "prove," the following, but based on circumstantial evidence, the likelihood is that it contains some measure of truth, but only the Lord knows everything.

I don't believe Nguyen Thi My-Duyen was kidnapped. When I failed to make the original trip to Vietnam due to Manisha's illness, I believe Anne, fearing the mother might change her mind, or perhaps another parent's referral fell through, gave my child to someone else.

Perhaps Anne thought I would never come to Vietnam. My documents were on the verge of expiring anyway. She also probably didn't want to risk the baby not being adopted. I'm sure there was a monetary component involved, and she didn't want to lose the several thousands of dollars that would go into her pocket. A baby was available and that was all that mattered. She was willing to take the risk and deal with the consequences later.

Even if I showed up on her doorstep at some point, she could explain away my referral—after all, I had already been through four—just offer me another child. What difference would it make as long as I got "any child"? People have lots of ways to justify wicked schemes.

I believe when I arrived and Anne had been unable to find a replacement baby, she made up the story about the kidnapping. She probably could have gotten away with it, except Jenni and I put the notice in the paper. She was already under investigation by the U.S. Embassy for baby selling and forgery of documents. Putting the ad in a public place would have put her at risk of having her license pulled as an adoption facilitator either by the U.S. Embassy or the Vietnamese government.

The police would have been called in for a missing person that really wasn't missing, and once someone told the mother, she would have reported that her baby was placed with another family. Anne would have been caught in a scam and subject to prosecution.

That brings up Joy. After eight years, when I was emotionally able to go back through her adoption papers, which I had saved but refused to look at, I found the name and phone number of a family in the medical documents. On a whim I called the number, and the woman who answered the phone was the same one as in the documents.

The lady explained to me that her husband had gone to Vietnam, worked with Anne as the facilitator, and on the way to Vietnam, the child they were going to adopt "disappeared," or was "no longer available," in the adoptive mother's words (a strange coincidence). Instead, they were offered three children. Joy was one of those children. Her husband traveled alone and she stayed behind with a child they had already adopted from Vietnam. She also told me in no uncertain terms that Anne had lied to them about "things."

When her husband saw that "Joy," was sickly, he decided to adopt one of the other children who appeared healthier. The family never came to adopt two children. They only came to adopt one and ended up adopting a different child.

So why did Joy wait all those months without being adopted? And why did Anne feel like she had to lie to me about why Joy was available? I don't know the truth where Anne is concerned, but I believe Joy was meant to be my daughter all along. God prevented her from being adopted by anyone else.

I put the question out there, though, if a family did adopt a little girl, Nguyen Thi My Duyen, born on July 15, 1996, and were in Hanoi, Vietnam, in October or November, 1999, I would love to know. I would like to believe that the beautiful little girl was adopted by a "forever" family that loves her.

Of course, as we know with Abbey, Anne redid and altered documents and birth certificates for expediency. Little Thi My Duyen may not have the same name, same birth date, or even the same birth certificate. So I probably will never know the truth until I arrive in heaven, but I do have peace because God has shown me that Thi My Duyen was adopted by someone and not kidnapped.

EPILOGUE

...the children of the promise

Romans 9:8

"I took away her dreams," my husband told the judge on September 4, 1986. Humanly speaking, he might have thought so. In John 8:44, Satan is described as the "Father of lies." Satan's desire was to destroy me, to make me doubt God's love and goodness. In my pain, I believed a lie, much like the children believed Aslan was dead in *The Lion, the Witch, and the Wardrobe.*

But there is a higher law, a law that governs the universe, that supersedes every human sin and evil that attempts to corrupt God's perfection. Our heavenly Father, who is full of grace and mercy, works out His purposes despite the evil one that lurks in the shadows. No human being has the power to thwart God's ultimate plan. He works in spite of the prince of this world and uses everything for His glory. Nothing is ever wasted, whether it is disease, affliction, corruption, greed, lies, or betrayal. Jesus is our ultimate example of being perfect and commanded us in Matthew 5:48 to "Be perfect, even as your heavenly Father in heaven is perfect."

God's incredible love for us is even more astounding when one considers He was under no obligation to adopt us. He could have treated us as angels, making us spiritually alive through regeneration, and justifying us under the law through His death and resurrection.[12] But to adopt us and

---

[12] Wayne Grudem, *Systematic Theology* (Grand Rapids, Mich, 1994), 738-739.

call us His children, to call Himself our Father, displays an intimacy in our relationship that defies, in my limited understanding, all logic. Why would the Creator of the universe want to be our Father? Even Albert Einstein, for all his genius, could not understand God as a personal God.[13]

Just as I signed a contract and made a down payment to adopt my children before I left for Nepal and Vietnam, God has given us "His Spirit as a deposit, guaranteeing what is to come" (2 Corinthians 1:22).

On July 26, 2000, we made a memorable trip to the Alachua County Courthouse to finalize Joy's adoption. A few years earlier, I had taken Manisha to the same place to finalize hers. Both of my children's adoption decrees are now sealed and kept safe, just as my adoption paper is sealed in heaven, waiting for Jesus to open and reveal my inheritance.

I renamed my children Hope and Joy, and God promises to give us a new name, "known only to him who receives it" (Rev 2:17). The adoption of my children represents a foreshadowing of what God has in store for all of us.

Much of the meaning of being a child of God has yet to be revealed because it's in the future. It is hard to comprehend the King giving me heavenly possessions that will never break, become outdated, cost too much, get lost, or that I don't have to return because they are defective. In my limited understanding, I have tried to imagine a world where there will be "no more death or mourning or crying or pain" (Rev 21:4); where the dwelling of God will be among us and He will wipe away every tear (Rev 21:4); where every kind of precious stone forms the foundation of the heavenly city which is paved in gold (Rev 21:19).

How can we envision perfection when all we have known is imperfection? God longs to be our Father, to share

---

[13] Hugh Ross, Ph.D., *The Creator and the Cosmos* (Colorado Springs,Col:Navpress, 2001), 75.

His inheritance with us, just as I longed to be an orphan's mother. God planned us to be part of His family from the foundations of the world. He made us for His glory and "set eternity in the hearts of men" (Ecc 3:11). He will give us new bodies that will never grow old or die, but will be raised imperishable (I Cor 15:42).

I am sure if I told my children, "You can go back to Vietnam or Nepal and live your former way of life before I adopted you," they would turn it down. Why would they want to go back to depravity and worms and hunger? In our heavenly home, the old order of things will have passed away (Rev 21:4) and the former things will not be remembered (Isaiah 65:17).

Before I adopted my two beautiful daughters, it was hard to imagine what it would like to be a mother. I dreamed about little girls and birthday parties, Christmas trees and toys, bear hugs and butterfly kisses, and my name transformed into the magical word "Mommy." Through prayer and God's faithfulness, what seemed impossible became real. And so it will be someday with us and our heavenly Father.

Hebrews 11:1 says that "Faith is being sure of what we hope for and certain of what we do not see." God knows how we are formed and remembers we are dust (Psalm 103:14). Jesus said when we pray, to call God "Our Father." The Spirit testifies with our spirit that we are God's children (Romans 8:16). God compares Himself to a father having compassion on his children. (Psalms 103:13). Our heavenly Father loved us so much that He gave us His only begotten Son (John 3:15), and He has made us heirs of God and co-heirs with Christ (Romans 8:17). Even creation itself will be liberated when we are brought into the glorious freedom of the children of God (Romans 8:21). Through adoption, God gave me my "Children of Dreams" and quenched the desires of my heart (Psalms 37:4). With God, our heavenly

Father, before the foundations of the world, He made us His "Children of Promise."[14]

Revelation 5: 9-10

9 Here is the new song they sang.
"You are worthy to take the scroll
and break open its seals.
You are worthy because you were put to death.
With your blood you bought people for God.
They come from every tribe, language, people and nation.
10 You have made them members of a royal family.
You have made them priests to serve our God.
They will rule on the earth."

---

[14] Romans 9:8 and Galatians 4:28

**Manisha's Referral
Picture February 1994**

Gypsy 1963

**Manisha in Nepal during
adoption April-May 1994**

Manisha's arrival on Mother's Day 1994

Joy at the Sofitel Metropole pool December 1999

Joy Christmas Eve in Hanoi December 1999

The Giving and Receiving Ceremony December 1999

Joy's arrival at the Jax Airport January 2000

Jenni somewhere in Alaska 2008

Joy and Abbey (Thi My-Sa) San Antonio in March 2009

Joy and Manisha in March 2009

Joy, Lorilyn and Manisha in April 2009

You can visit Lorilyn Roberts' website at
http://lorilynroberts.com

Photographs and Illustrations

Front cover photograph courtesy of Jenni Murphy. Used by permission.

Back cover photograph taken by author at Khari Dhunga, Janakpur Zone, near Chirokot in Eastern Nepal. The mounds are magnesite mines of Khari, meaning white, soft rocks. The mountain in the background is Kalinchok. This panoramic spot in the Himalayans is fifty-four miles east of Kathmandu and about nine thousand feet above sea level.

Nepal and Vietnam maps courtesy of Thomas Roberts: pages 11 and 134. Used by permission.

CPSIA information can be obtained at www.ICGtesting.com
Printed in the USA
LVOW12s1759110414

381360LV00002B/389/P